HOPE
In
PRESENT DANGER

HOPE
In
PRESENT DANGER

A TRUE STORY
SPERANTZA ADRIANA PASOS

HOPE IN PRESENT DANGER

This story is an account of an actual event. No composite anecdotes or other fiction techniques have been used. To protect privacy, however, some names have been changed.

ISBN 978-0-615-40440-0
ISBN 0-615-40440-5

Library of Congress Control Number: 2010917377

Printed in the United States of America
By Bethany Press International, Bloomington, MN

Cover design by Samuel Alicea
Interior text design by Mark Decker

First Edition

For copies of this book or speaking engagements, contact us at
www.hopeinpresentdanger.com.

DEDICATION

To the most amazing woman I know—my mother, my hero—
Michaela, and my father, Corneliu, whose love and sacrifice
have altered the course of my life.

I love you both
with all my heart!

CONTENTS

ACKNOWLEDGEMENTS

Ronald Karpiuk—your heart and generosity have made *Hope In Present Danger* possible. How can I ever thank you?

Martin Butler, Lee Bennett, Lorraine Lester, Sarah McGuire and Gladys Neigel—for your professional expertise and countless hours of proofreading and editing this manuscript. How can I ever repay you for such a gargantuan task? I am forever grateful.

Samuel Alicea—your creativity and passion for excellence have captured the essence of this story in an amazing way. You have blessed me beyond measure through your talent and generosity. I cannot thank you enough.

Emily Paul—your encouragement and enthusiasm have been the fuel that kept me going to the finish line. With all my heart, I thank you.

Cornelia Scribner, my wonderful sister—I could not have done this without you! You were my courage when the journey seemed impossible and were my strength when mine was fading. You have inspired me immensely and gave me hope to see this project through. Thank you for being such a priceless gift.

Ronnie, my husband and man I truly admire—for your dedication, your patience and your love toward me during this arduous process. You have encouraged me, sustained me and reminded me I must never give up. You are my rock and constant in my life. Thank you for imagining with me what I only dreamt possible.

Gabriella and Evangelina, my sweet girls—you are my treasures and my joy. Thank you for always cheering Mommy on. Don't ever forget to stand for what is right, even if you must stand alone.

To all those who have touched my life and have inspired me to complete this project—to all of you, I am forever grateful.

GOD—without whom none of this would have been possible. You are my eternal inspiration, sustainer and my hope.

THE PLAN

Chapter 1

H e made it! He made it! He's alive!" With those words, my father dropped the phone, collapsed to the ground, and began crying uncontrollably. Shocked, I stood there, my heart pounding faster and faster as my mind began jumping to frightening conclusions.

"Tata, what happened?" I asked. "Who's alive?"

"Who could have been in such danger? And, if they're alive, why is my father weeping?" I wondered. I glanced toward Mother only to see that she, too, was sobbing. Dismayed, I felt my heart sink.

"What could possibly be so wrong?" I thought. "And why won't they tell me anything?"

After what seemed like an eternity, my parents motioned for me to sit down. Scared, I lowered myself to the ground and squeezed in between them. And for the very first time in my life, I heard them whisper to me the incredible plan my family orchestrated to escape Communist Romania in search of freedom.

Hidden behind the Iron Curtain and severed from the world, my beautiful country was dying slowly from the blow of Communism. Nestled between the Carpathian Mountains, the Blue Danube, and the Black Sea, what had been a thriving kingdom known as the "Grainery of Central Europe" just thirty years earlier, had now become a country in mourning—a country of rations and portions, where people stood in line for hours in hope of receiving one loaf of bread.

The Securitate was working in full force. Patterned with diabolical precision after the Russian KGB, this state-controlled agency received its orders directly from the Soviet Union, and used the same methods of emotional, moral and physical torture and intimidation.

Christians were persecuted for their beliefs; telephones were tapped; the media was biased, and there was no freedom of speech. Anyone who spoke against the government was immediately incarcerated or killed.

If one believed in God, that person was considered a traitor. If one chose not to belong to the Communist Party, that person was labeled anti-partisan and suffered the economic, financial, emotional and physical brunt of such a choice. Dictator Nicolae Ceaușescu's grip upon the people and the country was tightening every day, and freedom had become a figment of one's imagination.

"Sweetheart," Mother said, "Uncle Emil was pressured to become an informant, a secret agent for the Securitate. They wanted him to work for them. They wanted Uncle to spy on the Christians in Alba Iulia."

"I need a couple days to think about this," he had told them. If he would have refused them outright, he would have endangered his family. So, he chose, instead, to risk his own life and swim across the Danube into Yugoslavia. For an entire week, we didn't know if he was dead or alive, until just minutes ago. Darling, we couldn't tell you anything before. It was too dangerous. But now you must listen carefully."

"What next?" I asked, as my heart raced.

"Sperantza," Mother said, "it's only a matter of days until the government finds out what has happened. Once they do, our lives will be in danger. We must escape, and we must do it fast."

"What? Escape the Securitate? Mama, how can we do that? Uncle Emil swam across the Danube, but what about us? How can we do it?" I heard my voice get louder and louder, as the tension inside of me became painfully obvious.

"Shh!" Mother motioned, pressing a finger to her lips.

Father got up from the floor and turned the radio on louder than before. It was a small safety measure my parents always took before telling me something important, in case the house was bugged. The words—danger, death, escape—were playing in my mind over and over again, like a broken record and I felt my head begin to spin. Danger, death, escape... Danger, death, escape...danger....

"Do you remember when Mother and I applied for a trip to Germany, but we were denied the Visas?" continued Father.

"Of course," I said, clearly remembering Mr. Enescu, our neighbor, who worked for the Criminal Justice System, coming and speaking with my parents.

"Mr. Enescu wanted to intervene for us," said Father, "but we asked him not to. He wanted to put in a 'good word' on our behalf with the Securitate. 'I know you won't defect, Mr. Totpal,' he said. 'I know you'll come back.' We told him we had prayed for this trip and would accept God's will for us.

Sperantza, if we would have allowed him to intervene for us, his career would have been finished. His life, and that of his family, would have been in extreme danger. Mr. Enescu would have been considered an accomplice to our defection."

"Is that the reason you didn't go on that trip?"

"Yes, darling, that's why."

"So, what do we do now?"

"We have applied for a trip to Turkey for you and Mother. If they give their approval, you two will be leaving within weeks."

"Wait a minute... What about you? What about my sister?" I asked.

"We must remain behind, Sperantza," said my father, sadness creasing his face. "They would never allow all of us to leave."

"Tata, Turkey, of all places? And without you, or Cornelia?"

At only fourteen, the thought of not only my own life and Mother's, but that of my father and little sister hanging in the balance was just too much for me to bear. No matter how hard I tried to stop the tears, the flood of emotions overwhelmed me and I began to sob.

"Shh. Don't cry, Sperantza. Don't cry. God will take care of us. He will protect us, and He will make a way. You must be brave, my child. You must help your mother. And above all, you must keep the secret."

Chapter 2

Even though exhausted, I couldn't sleep much that night. My mind kept racing, jumping from question to question. "Will they give us the approval? What if they refuse? What happens then? What if we get caught? How will we get out?"

On and on it went. Those same three words—danger, death, escape— kept ringing in my ears as if haunting me, and I could not shake them off, no matter how hard I tried.

Perhaps for some, the thought of traveling abroad would have been a dream come true; but, for me, it felt more like a nightmare. I grew up as a privileged, somewhat sheltered child. Even though my family was Christian in a Communist country, we didn't lack economic means.

My parents owned and ran a successful photography studio near the city of Brașov, a ski haven for foreign tourists. They also owned a house in the city, had their own car, and traveled extensively throughout the country due to the nature of their business. We often took vacations at the Black Sea and the Carpathian Mountains. Weekends were spent at my grandparents' villa in Breaza.

By American standards, owning a business, a car, and a home may be the norm, but in a Communist country like Romania, it was the exception, certainly not the rule.

Considering, an intellectual was paid an average of about 3,000 lei or $30 a month, and a car cost between 70,000 and 80,000 lei—more than the salary for two years—owning a car was an impossibility for most, especially because there was no monthly-payment option. Purchasing a brand new car required cold cash. But one couldn't simply go to a dealer, pay the money, and walk out with a car. The person would be placed on a waiting list for months, often even years.

Owning a home was also an incredible achievement. The majority lived in tenement-like buildings made of pre-cast concrete. These square-like monolithic boxes looked as though they had been cut out of the same mold and painted with the same color—gray. Everywhere one looked, there they stood. Rows and rows of ugly, dirt-like, monotone gray. Inside, the living quarters were tiny, with kitchens so narrow that a six-month pregnant woman couldn't enter sideways.

As similar thoughts continued flooding my mind, the reality of leaving it all behind was slowly sinking in. The comforts of my home, my family, my friends, my belongings, my school, my church, would all be gone. I would leave it all behind—everything I had, everything I knew, and everyone I loved—exchanging the all too familiar for the fearful unknown. And all for the simple reason of having been born in a Communist country and believing in God.

As the sun's first rays lightly kissed my face, my mother's voice interrupted my thoughts. Groggily, I opened my eyes.

"Please hurry, Sperantza. Get ready quickly. Today, we have an audience with your school principal and school board."

"Oh, no," I silently groaned as I flopped back on my pillow. Not my school. Please, not there. I never want to go there again. "Why do we need to see them, Mama? Why do I have to go and face those people again? I can't, I just can't," my voice cracked.

"I know it's hard for you, my child," said my mother, her voice, full of compassion, "but just this once. I pray to God this will be the last time you'll have to see them."

I wasn't quite so sure. For five long years, I had faced my persecutors. From the tender age of nine, students and teachers alike ridiculed me and made me the brunt of their jokes, simply because I was a Christian. I had already graduated and taken my high school placement exam at a different school.

"Why do I have to go back there again?" I asked.

"Honey, because you are a minor, the government requires not only your parents' permission but also that of your school principal. As a citizen under the Communist regime, they will determine whether or not you are deemed 'worthy' to travel abroad. They will base their decisions on your grades but most of all on your behavior, Sperantza."

"Well, then, I'm doomed," I thought. My grade in Character and Behavior was not an A like all other arduous students. It was a B, and, for a girl especially, that was reason enough for denial.

After Mama drilled me with possible questions and instructed me on how to answer, we were finally on our way. Within minutes, we arrived in the parking lot facing my school complex. I felt my stomach turn as we approached the building. It was June, and school was no longer in session.

As we entered and walked down the long, gray, concrete corridor, the only sound I heard was that of our shoes hitting the floor. Everything felt so strange. "I'm not afraid, I'm not afraid, I'm not afraid," I kept repeating to myself. Yet, I still felt my heart pounding faster and faster.

Keeping my eyes fixed on the principal's wooden double glass door at the end of the hallway, I prayed: "Jesus, help me, please! Give me the right answers and help me not to be afraid."

But as I got closer, flashbacks of that awful day roared back with a vengeance. I felt as though I was walking in slow motion, transported as it were, in a time capsule. Soon, everything around me began to blur. The feelings of helplessness and despair were as fresh and familiar as the day it happened, and all of a sudden I was back in her classroom again.

Chapter 3

Sestraș!" said my math teacher, with a smirk on her face. "To the blackboard."

I froze. Had she really called me up or had I only imagined it? Because I was a believer and she, a hard-nosed Communist, she hated me with a passion. School was taught six-days a week and I didn't attend class on Saturdays. My friends had warned me about her. She had intimidated me throughout the year, but had now declared open war by telling the class what she would do to me if I continued missing school on Saturdays.

"I prohibit you to give her any of your notes," she had instructed them. "I forbid you to help her. Anyone who does will suffer severe consequences. I'll make her give up that god of hers," she said. "I'll show her who's really god—Ceaușescu! Ceaușescu!"

"Sestraș!" she said, her voice rising this time, snapping me out of my daze.

"Can't you hear me? To the blackboard, I said."

Finding a small sliver of strength, I pushed myself up from my desk and slowly walked to the blackboard. I could almost feel my classmates' stares boring into me. I picked up the large compass with my trembling hands and started to draw the angles she had called for with the instrument. I felt the chalk shift in the compass, but I was so scared I couldn't say a word. As I drew the lines, I prayed they would be correct. When I finally finished, I glanced at her with a small sparkle of hope in my eyes. Maybe, just maybe, she would help me. She certainly could see that the compass was faulty.

Her eyes locked into mine as if almost turning to stone. The smirk on her face briefly returned just long enough for me to imagine what grade I would receive. I realized I had been set up when the student she called next to the blackboard requested a different compass. The following words she spoke were like a punch in the stomach, whose pain never went away.

"Go sit down!" she hissed. "You have a 3."

A gasp filled the room as I struggled to catch my breath. A "3"? A "4" was an F, but a 3 was off the charts! In all other subjects I was a straight A student. I had never failed at anything before. Turning as red as a beet, I stumbled back to my seat and buried my head in my hands. I didn't even hear when the teacher announced, "class dismissed."

Chapter 4

Sperantza, are you feeling all right?"

"Hm? Uh, I'm fine Mama. I'm fine," I responded, as reality gripped me again.

"Are you sure? You look so pale," she said.

I felt her arm pull me into the restroom.

"Here, wash your face and drink some water. You must pull yourself together, my child. Regain your composure!"

"I know, Mama, I know. It's just that... I saw her, I saw my math teacher again."

"There is no one else here, Sperantza, no one but you and me."

"But it was so real, Mama. I'm telling you I was there in the classroom. I saw the blackboard. I heard her voice."

"I know what you've endured. What I don't want you to forget, though, is that God is on our side and He is more powerful than anyone who'd want to harm us."

That's what Mother always said: "God is on our side—always, anytime, anywhere." Deep down in my heart, I knew she was right, but it still didn't take away the pain I felt.

"Are you ready? We must go in now."

"Citizen Totpal. What brings you here?" said the principal.

"Good morning, sir. We need your permission for our daughter to travel to Turkey on an excursion we have applied for," said Father, handing him the papers. "We need your approval and your signature, sir."

"Will you be going along, Citizen Totpal?"

"Oh, no, sir. It's just my daughter and my wife. It's a present for her 8th grade graduation."

"She's an exceptional student. And that's quite a present. But all that knowledge is worthless, unless, of course, she changes her mind regarding this religion of hers. You know all university entrance exams are administered on Saturdays. Why don't you let her go to school like any other normal child? Don't you realize you're ruining her future?" he said, motioning to Father, shaking the papers in his hand.

"I realize that, sir, but this is her choice. We have never forced the issue. This was always her decision."

Back and forth they went, my dad and the principal, as if I didn't even exist.

"My father is right," I heard myself suddenly say. "This is my decision. My parents had nothing to do with it, sir."

"Well, young lady, you will never amount to much as long as you continue on this crazy path of yours. Does sweeping the streets sound inviting to you?" he asked, raising his voice, lifting up his hands in the air as if exasperated with my choice.

"Because a street-sweeper is what you'll end up being if you don't go to a university. That's what you'll be—just a street sweeper."

I lowered my head. Under the Communist regime, a job wasn't just a job. There was prestige that came along with what you did, and a street-sweeper was considered to be the lowest of the low.

"Give up your education," he continued, "give up your status in society, give up your future, for what? Just for believing in something that doesn't even exist? I don't understand. I just don't understand."

And then, as if an outside force impressed him, he continued, "I'll sign these papers for you. I believe this trip will do you some good; help you think about what I said. Stop thinking about nonsense religion! Think about your future instead! And give up on that god of yours!"

With those words, he handed the papers to Father, turned around, walked towards his desk and sat down. Dismissed with approval in hand, we left his office in amazement. He had signed them after all. No doubt, a power far beyond human was at work within that man. Mother was right. God was on our side, but as I was soon to find out, the struggle had just begun.

Chapter 5

Is this all we need?" I naively asked. "They haven't told us, but I'm sure we'll need our passports," said Mother. "The militia holds them for "safe keeping." We're not allowed to have them in our possession except when we travel. They take all kinds of measures to imprison us, Sperantza."

Mother was right. We couldn't openly worship God. We couldn't speak against the government. We couldn't listen to short-wave radio for fear of being imprisoned. Our television had only one channel. The programming was mostly in the evenings for just a few hours and filled with propaganda. On the weekends, it was a bit more extensive, but everything that was presented had to be verified and pre-approved by the government. Every piece of information that was disseminated to the public was first questioned, planned, and controlled. The few newspapers sold in the entire country, all contained the same Communist indoctrination.

Everything we did was monitored by the government, the Securitate, and the KGB. Someone once said that the greatest measure of a country can be assessed by the number of people who want in and the number of people who want out. We were prisoners in our own country. We were kept in by force, certainly not by choice.

Now, the passports. We couldn't even hold our own passports. They were held for us.

"What's next?" I thought.

And as if Mother could read my mind, she said, "What's left for us to do now is pray and wait. Wait for the answer, hope for the approval, and pray the government doesn't make the connection between our three families."

I heard a deep sigh. Then silence.

After a long while, I finally dared to ask the question: "Auntie Lia and Uncle Nicu are not coming back either, are they?"

"No, they're not, sweetheart."

Mother's words began to make more sense now. My other aunt and uncle had left on an excursion to Austria just four weeks before.

"They're due to come back within a matter of days," Mother continued, and therein lies the danger. If we don't get the approval for our trip before they are due back, the government will obviously become suspicious. If they turn themselves in to the Austrian Government and request Political Asylum, that will also place us in jeopardy, because the Romanian Government will find out."

"What will they do, then?"

"Their plan is to wait as long as possible before turning themselves in, in hopes it will buy us enough time."

"What about Uncle Emil?"

"Uncle Emil has already requested Political Asylum in Italy. It's only a matter of time before the government will find out he has defected. Once they do, Sperantza, they will be on high alert."

I didn't understand what "high alert" meant, but it didn't sound good.

"High alert," Mother continued, "means the government would begin an in-depth search for all possible family members connected with those defectors. They would immediately inform all travel channels to be on high alert and block any possibility of escape. Our names would be given to various government entities that would be on the lookout for us. Any form of transportation would then become even more dangerous for us. Sperantza, the trains and buses are infiltrated with Securitate agents. Of course, if we were to drive our own car, we would have to get through the militia checkpoints that are everywhere."

I had seen those checkpoints on the side of the road. I was all-too-familiar with them. Every time we traveled to and from my grandparents' house in Breaza to Braşov, there they were. Oh, how I hated them. Those weren't checkpoints—they were extortion points!

We would be traveling peacefully when, all of a sudden, out of nowhere, a militia would step out from one of those outposts, pull in front of our car, and flag us down.

I knew what came next.

They'd stop, search, and sanction us. My father would be told to get out of the car. Then, the interrogation would begin.

"Where are you coming from? Why were you there? Who did you see? Where are you going? What are you doing? Who's in your car?"

They'd look inside the car, check our trunk, and then continue on with their intimidation tactics. If they couldn't find any real reason to fine Father, they would make sure that they came up with one. That was their means of subsidizing their miserable salaries—by extortion.

These men had the power to do whatever they wanted with us. They could revoke my father's license for no reason. They could even confiscate our car. They could report us to the higher authorities by making false accusations. Whatever means they could employ to gain something for themselves, they would, and there was no system set in place that could protect us. The system itself was putridly corrupt.

In the end, it always came down to an exchange. Father would reach down in his pocket and pull out the amount of money they demanded in exchange for his papers and the right to continue driving on with his family.

Oh, how I resented those militia men who had such power over us. I wouldn't dare imagine what would happen if the government gave them a real reason to hunt us down. Without a doubt, this time, the exchange wouldn't just be money. The price to pay would be much higher.

Drained, I made my way to my room and collapsed on my bed. It had been a long day. Still thinking about the future, I heard Mother enter the room. As she kissed me goodnight, I held her hand tightly and asked, "Mama, when will we know if they know about Auntie Lia and Uncle?"

"We won't, my child. We just have to trust God, and pray. Pray that somehow He blinds them so they will let us go."

Chapter 6

Two weeks later we were still praying... still waiting... Hours away from our scheduled trip to Turkey, we had yet to hear anything from the officials.

Mother and Father were still hopeful, but I had my doubts. It was already one o'clock in the afternoon. The bus was scheduled to leave from Cîmpina, a city not too far from my grandparents' home in Breaza, at six o'clock the next morning. Although we lived in Braşov, we had applied for this trip in Cîmpina, in the hopes it would make it harder for the government to make the connection.

"More than likely, we were denied the visas," I sighed. "But if we were, why hadn't they told us yet? And, if they knew about my aunt and uncles, why hadn't they called us in for questioning? Do they want to entrap us? Do they want to arrest us in front of everybody tomorrow and make an example for all to see?" I felt my heart pounding faster and faster, as the questions bombarded my head. Nonetheless, my parents decided we would go and spend the night at my grandparents' home. It was almost 2:00 PM when we drove up to their villa on Plevnei 7 in Breaza.

Set at the end of a hundred-meter driveway, the villa was barely visible from the street. Lined by a variety of fruit trees that formed a luscious green canopy, this was my special haven. In spite of my previous worries, all my concerns drifted away, if only for a moment, as we drove down that gorgeous driveway and looked at the surroundings.

There were Jonathan, green and yellow apple trees; D'Anjou pear trees, peach trees, red and yellow plum trees, and several prune trees. They even had a fig tree, which was quite unusual because Romania's weather was quite severe and figs generally thrived in much warmer climates.

But Buni, as I affectionately called my grandmother, was an amazing woman and an incredibly talented gardener. Everything she touched turned into beauty and bounty, from the fruit trees to the flowers, to the house. She loved spending time outdoors tending her garden.

Nearing the house, the driveway opened up to a huge semi-circle, lined by lush green bushes shaped with precision against the fence. A few feet further, a breathtaking rose garden of deep burgundy, blood-red, blush pink, bright yellow, and cheerful burnt orange buds opened up to the sun, emanating the most wonderful scent. On both sides of the steps that led to the house were two hot pink Oleanders and large Agave plants. A beautiful black wrought iron bench and several chaise lounges sat on the manicured lawn.

Ten granite semi-circular steps led to the front entrance of an all-glass veranda overlooking the immense driveway. As one stepped inside, it was as if entering a mini-botanical garden. From pink hortensias to philodendrons; from red mums to African violets, the room seeped euphoria. In the center stood a large glass-covered table surrounded by comfortable armchairs. A French door led into the spacious living room where a 12-foot-high oil painting of Christ's removal from the Cross bade visitors to come in.

A two-story home with blue French louvers and a balcony overlooking the garden, the house sat on a lot larger than the length of a football field.

It had four spacious rooms with central heat, a full bathroom, two large walk-in pantries, a large hallway and a spacious cellar. Behind the house, there was a separate building that held our summer kitchen and a warehouse for storage. In the middle of the back yard stood a well and a gigantic walnut tree with branches that covered nearly a third of the house and a large portion of the back yard. Among the nearly 100 fruit trees, there were also Black and Rainier Cherry Trees.

This was the place I loved and cherished, the place where my most precious childhood memories were made.

Chapter 7

Located in the Muntenia Region of Romania, a very fertile place with valleys and gently-rolling green hills, Breaza was a favorite among Government officials. This resort-like town was the place where many of the prime-ministers and parliamentarians owned summer residences.

The fact that my grandparents were even able to acquire a property in such a place was a direct blessing from God. Especially because between 1943 and 1944 during the massive deportations from the German-occupied territories to the concentration camps, my grandfather, who worked as a railroad chief engineer, risked his own life and that of his family to save nearly 500 Jews, brought in from Hungary. Running as the presidential candidate for the Romanian Social Democratic Party four years later, he openly opposed the Communist forces.

Having been warned, however, by a former colleague, that the Communist Party was already undermining the elections and planned to eradicate all opposing parties through death or imprisonment, he was forced to renounce his candidacy. The Communist Party, which, ironically promised equality to all, later installed the infamous dictator, Nicolae Ceaușescu, who terrorized Romania with an iron fist until his death in December, 1989.

Although oppressed by the Securitate all his life for refusing to become a Communist Party member, God protected and blessed my grandfather beyond measure. With the money he received when he retired from his job at the Romanian National Railroad Company, along with the proceeds of the sale of his previous property and his inheritance, he was able to acquire what Buni later named Villa Betel.

When Grandfather discovered it, it was in disarray. The wife of the former proprietor had passed away and the large property had been left unattended for some time. Their efforts, along with Buni's love for beauty and art, transformed the place into a piece of heaven.

As we pulled up and got out of the car, Grandfather welcomed us with a hug and a kiss.

"The officials just called, Michaela. Your excursion has been approved! You're leaving tomorrow morning at six o'clock."

As he said that, a small figure dashed towards Mother. Picking her up, Mama twirled her around. A beautiful little girl with curly, chestnut-colored hair, my little sister, Cornelia, was only four years old. I wondered how Mama must have felt embracing her, knowing that she would leave her behind in just hours.

Suddenly, I felt my knees begin to knock. I was experiencing such an unrealistic mix of emotions—excited about the endless possibilities, but so overwhelmed at the same time. This was it. In less than sixteen hours, we would actually be leaving my beloved country, Romania, for good. I only prayed we would succeed.

The rest of the afternoon and evening were like a fog. The only thing I clearly remember was something Father did. From the camera we were to take with us, he pulled out the film, and then carefully inserted 300 Deutsch Marks inside the spool. Slowly, he loaded the film back into the camera and handed it to Mother.

"You must be careful with this, darling," he said. "You can only imagine what would happen to you if they found it."

THE ESCAPE

Chapter 8

I t's time to wake up, Sperantza," I heard Buni say. Slowly, I opened my eyes, though they were still heavy. I knew I had to get up, but all I wanted to do was snuggle under the covers and push the world away. I got dressed and joined my parents and grandparents on the veranda, where we gathered around the large table to pray.

I will never forget Grandfather's words, "Doamne Isuse, apărăle şi nu le lăsa...." Father, protect them and don't leave them, please. Bring them to liberty and safety, and give us peace. Remain with us and help us to see them again. Amen."

I had heard how Grandfather had suffered much during the Communist regime. That could explain why he was so stern and rarely showed emotion. I had never seen him cry, but there were tears in his eyes that morning as he embraced Mother and kissed us goodbye.

"Dumnezeu cu voi." May God be with you, he said. "God be with you."

Buni was crying. Father was crying. As I turned around, I saw Mother was crying too, as she walked towards the bed where my baby sister lay sleeping peacefully, completely oblivious of the eminent danger her family faced. Oh, to be a child, to trust, to just not even know...

As Mother bent over to kiss my little sister's angelic face, I saw tears flowing down her cheeks. In that kiss was so much love, yet so much pain. Love, because Mama knew that, as Christians, the only way to freely worship God meant leaving our country. And pain, because Mama knew a four-year-old would never understand the price of freedom.

As she kissed her rosy cheeks and perfectly round head, she ran her fingers through her silky hair. Then she just stood there, gazing at her, as if she wanted an imprint of her tiny countenance.

What must have gone through her heart or mind I couldn't comprehend, until the day when I, myself, was blessed with my firstborn. I had once read that making the decision to have a child was momentous because it meant deciding to have your heart walk outside your body, forever! I realized then, and continue discovering to this day that my heart belongs to me no longer, but to the ones who are a part of me forever.

Kissing my grandparents goodbye, we entered the car. As Father drove away, I felt butterflies in my stomach. It was such a glorious day, pregnant with hope and expectation, yet at the same time fear. The sun was shining brightly, and the dew was glistening on the green grass, giving it a tint of silver. Passing the rows of gorgeous flowers and majestic trees, and finally leaving the gates of Villa Betel behind, I wondered whether I would ever see this peaceful place again.

As I rolled down my window to wave goodbye for the last time, I caught one last glimpse of my grandparents. Buni, covered with her large terra-cotta shawl, trying hard to keep smiling, stood next to Grandfather and waved slowly as if to say, "We love you. We love you. Our love goes with you."

The ride from Breaza to Cîmpina wasn't long, perhaps 15-20 minutes at most. I don't remember any of the conversation. I was silent, almost introspective. Arriving at the coach bus station, we entered the waiting area and were told that embarkation would not take place for another 30 minutes. I was hungry. Dad went to get us some gogoși (Romanian-style donuts made of sweet fried dough bread, dipped in vanilla powdered sugar). As I watched the people come into the waiting room, I glanced at my surroundings.

The room was decorated with poster scenes from countries throughout Europe. As I gazed at them, I could only wonder what it would feel like to visit some of those places.

"What is taking Tata so long?" I finally asked Mother.

"He probably couldn't find anything open yet," she said. "He may have gone to a store further down the street. Don't worry, he'll be back soon. We still have time."

Just as she finished saying those words, a young, very pregnant lady, who I later found out was to be our tour guide, announced that we would be embarking our bus immediately.

"What about Tata?" I asked, shocked. "Mama, he's still not here!"

Mother squeezed my hand, a signal for me to be quiet, a silent reminder we were being watched. I remembered Dad had warned me about the Securitate. Secret police agents were everywhere. The tour guide could have been one, or even the older man sitting across from us. One never knew.

I followed her lead and said nothing more. Within minutes we were seated in the bus. My eyes searched desperately for Father, expecting him to come at any moment.

"We are ready to depart," the tour guide announced.

"Mama, they're leaving ahead of schedule," I said.

Mother looked firmly at me, squeezing my hand even tighter. Looking through the back window, I saw Dad running desperately towards us, as the bus pulled away. I felt like screaming, "Stop! Stop the bus! Don't leave! You can't leave! I want to see my daddy! I want to hold him one last time! I want to hug him and kiss him goodbye!"

Yet I could not! Although I felt like dying inside, I couldn't even shed a tear. Any sign of emotion would have revealed our intent to defect, and that meant prison or death for my entire family. Feeling completely helpless, I cried and cried and cried, but not a sound escaped me. As I held all my emotions inside, I wondered if I'd ever see my father again. I wondered if we would truly escape our "living hell" and wondered what would happen if we didn't.

Was this the price of freedom? Was this the cost to worship God? My heart rushed back to the look on my father's heartbroken face as he watched the bus disappear upon the horizon.

"I want my daddy. I just want my daddy," I thought. "Hush, little heart. Be silent. Pay the price. Pay for loving One who loved you so much more."

As if she had read my mind and felt my pain, Mother caressed my hand ever so gently. She understood. She knew how difficult this was for me, still just a child, to handle such ordeal. And in a way only a mother could, she looked at me, calmed my fears and soothed my pain, without uttering a single word.

What I couldn't help wonder was what she must have felt. What thoughts were rushing through her head? I wondered if she, too, felt like crying. I wondered, but I couldn't even ask. Watching her pained but resolute expression, I understood this was the sacrifice our family had to make.

The tour guide seated behind us, who saw me waiving desperately to my father, said, matter-of-factly:

"Don't worry, darling, it's not like you'll never see him again. The trip is only five days long."

"Oh, if you only knew," I thought. "If you only knew."

Chapter 9

Within a few hours we reached the border with Bulgaria. After passing through Bucharest, the capital, we came to a full stop. Through my window, I could see men swarming around the bus; some in green, others in blue uniforms, yet others in civilian clothes. The men in blue held on to large, mean-looking dogs on leashes.

"Mama, why have we stopped?" I innocently asked.

"We're at the border, honey," she said. "They must check our papers." Several hours later, I realized they were checking much more than that.

Five corpulent men entered the bus. They were armed and held papers in their hands. Their uniforms made them seem even more imposing. They walked the length of the bus, staring at us as if searching for someone. As they scanned our faces, they would then look down at their papers again, only to stare back at our faces once again. Back and forth they walked through the bus aisle.

Their intimidation tactics worked well. Conversations ceased. Silence reigned.

"You! You, you, and you!" they barked, tearing through the silence. "Follow us!"

As I watched through my window, I saw those passengers follow the armed militia to the motor coach baggage compartment, where they were apparently told to identify their luggage. I saw them bend over, reach down, and pull out their bags onto the street pavement. The armed men opened their bags, emptied the contents onto the cement, and searched every compartment and crevice possible.

Once done, the dogs sniffed the bags and the passengers disappeared out of sight. After what seemed like a very long time, the men were escorted back into the bus, only to have the process begin all over again with the rest of us.

"They're ruthless," I thought. "These militia men carelessly tear bags open, throw belongings onto the ground and bark orders. They have no mercy. They show no kindness. They treat these people like animals, not like human beings. They must be looking for something. But why does it have to be that way?"

Breaking the silence, I finally whispered: "Mama, what are they looking for?"

"They're checking for contraband, any foreign currency, cigarettes, alcohol," she responded calmly.

All I could think about was our camera and the Deutsch Marks hidden there. "Oh, dear Lord, please don't let them find that money. Help us, Jesus," I breathed, silently.

I barely finished my prayer when I saw the tour guide, Mrs. Ionescu, head toward our seats. "Mrs. Totpal, they want you outside."

"Let's go," said Mother, grabbing my hand.

As I got up from my seat, I felt blood rushing to my head. I didn't know if my feet would hold me, but I followed Mother's footsteps. I know there must have been a Higher Power that steadied my pace as I got off of the bus that day.

"Good afternoon, Citizen Totpal. What are you bringing on this trip?"

"I have brought some cheese and some traditional folklore pieces of clothing to trade or to sell, gentlemen." (Since we were not allowed to hold any foreign currency, the Romanian government allowed us to bring items to sell or trade for Turkish goods.) "The rest are personal items for my daughter and me."

"Very well, then. Open your luggage!"

"Oh, God," I thought, "not the bag with the camera."

Mother calmly opened one of the bags. They casually looked inside, never removing any of the items like they had done to those before us, never searching the second bag.

"Thank you, madam, you may go back in the bus."

"Was that it?" I thought. "What had just happened?" These same men who had been so rude and rough with the others were kind to us. Whether they saw the camera or not, I will never know. What I do know is that God calmed my fears and gave me strength so that I wouldn't faint. He gave me courage not to cry, and He stopped those armed men from doing us harm.

Oh, what an awesome God I serve! One who understood and quieted my fears... One who comprehended my anxieties... and One who would not give me more than I could bear. Without a doubt, His angels were at work in those men because their behavior was so unlike anything I had seen.

Returning to our seats, we watched in amazement how, one by one, the rest of the passengers were interrogated and searched. Just when I thought we were ready to depart, two more armed men entered. I gasped. Not again! What were they searching for now?

It seemed as though they had smelled blood and were back on the hunt. This time, they didn't hesitate. With eyes fixed straight ahead, they marched directly to the back of the bus where a young man in his early twenties, holding onto a black and white plastic shoulder bag, was seated by himself.

"Citizen, is that all you're carrying on this trip?"

"Hmm, well, yea, yes, comrade."

With a sarcastic laugh, one of the men said to the other, "Isn't he a smart packer?"

"Yep. Ha, ha. The place where he's going, he won't even need that," the other responded.

Grabbing him roughly by his arms, they both yelled, "Get up! Let's go! You're coming with us."

The door closed slowly behind them as they left the coach, never to be seen again. I heard the sound of the engines revving as the bus driver turned the key.

Within minutes, Mrs. Ionescu said, "We are now ready to depart. I apologize for the delay. This will be a pleasant trip, I assure you. Just sit back and relax. We will be heading to Sofia, Bulgaria, where we will spend the night and the following day. We will then head to Istanbul. So, sit back, relax and soak in the beautiful scenery."

As the coach bus drove across the Romanian border into Bulgaria and beautiful music played softly in the background, my mind replayed the last scene over and over again. I wondered where they took that man. "What did they do to him? Did they torture him? Imprison him? Kill him? Through it all, I couldn't help but realize how incredibly blessed we were. It was only by God's grace that we weren't in his place," I thought quietly, not saying a word. I couldn't. Saying anything in such tight quarters would mean running the risk of being heard by someone. Anyone.

Father had warned me about those secret agents—Securitate as they called them. No one knew exactly who they were or how many of them were around. One feared everybody. Men and women, young and old could be informants. Even churches were infiltrated by them.

Many of our own neighbors in Brașov worked for the military, militia, and criminal justice system. The majority were informants. Most of them were young, recently married couples who didn't have much. Our home was the place they'd come when they needed something: money, advice, flour, sugar, potatoes, eggs, bread... anything. Mother and Father always gave

46

them what they needed, never asking for anything in return. Since they were photographers, my parents also took portrait pictures of their children and their families, never charging them a penny.

I remember one neighbor in particular, who worked for the militia. Recently married, Mr. Şerban began visiting our home regularly. Not once, not twice, but sometimes, three, four or five times in a day. He wouldn't even knock when he entered—he'd barge right in. If we were eating at the table, he'd come in, stare at our food, and make all kinds of comments.

"I wish I had your connections Mr. Totpal. Where did you get that from? Isn't that expensive?"

"Sit down Mr. Şerban. Come, join us. Have something to eat," my parents would say.

Oftentimes he would. After a while, he would just leave, only to return a few hours later for another round of questioning.

Besides the photography studio my parents had in the city, they had a photo processing laboratory at home. Mr. Şerban's apartment was exactly across the street from our house. From his balcony and any window, he could see if someone entered or exited our home. As a matter of fact, most of the families who lived in that apartment building facing our home worked for some branch of the secret police. Thus, our house was under constant surveillance.

Many times, when my parents were working on a project, we would hear the gate swing open and footsteps at the door. The door would open and in would come Mr. Şerban.

"How is the American today?" he'd sarcastically ask my father.

"Who do you have working for you now? Who are these people? Where did they come from? Let me see their ID's. Do they have the right to work? How much are you paying them? Oh, I see you have a new camera. What about that new light? Where did you get that from? It's hard to find those." On and on he would go.

Not only Mr. Şerban, but any of the neighbors could have turned us in, for no reason whatsoever. Just because we had things that they did not was reason enough.

But God's mercy and protection was ever present. Although living under Communist oppression, His blessing was still upon us as in the times of old when He had said: "Seek ye first, the kingdom of God and all these things shall be added unto you."

God kept true to His word and added more than we ever needed—He added enough for us to always give. Faithful to His promise, He had made us a blessing to many who intended to do us harm.

Chapter 10

I must have finally drifted into a deep sleep because when I awoke, it was already dusk. The sun was slipping quickly below the horizon, and the coach was pulling into what looked like a modern hotel.

"Did you sleep well?" Mother asked.

"Yes. How long did I sleep?"

"You must have been really tired, because you slept the whole way through."

"Are we in Sofia, already?"

"Yes, we've just arrived. The guide announced we'll be eating at the hotel. They'll assign us our rooms after dinner. We'll have a couple of hours to walk around and visit some shops, if you want."

"Yes, I would like that, Mama."

We got off the bus and followed the crowd into the restaurant. Stepping into the long, narrow room with large picture windows, we found a place to sit. The floor was covered with red carpet. White floral damask dressed the square tables. In the center of each, a small round vase held a bouquet of fresh roses.

Their fragrance brought me back to Breaza, wondering what Buni was doing now.... Was she outside watering her flower garden or inside kneeling by her bed, head covered with her brown shawl, praying for us, as she often did?

A deep man's voice snapped me back into reality, interrupting my thoughts: "The menu for tonight is matzo ball soup, Wiener schnitzel with mashed potatoes served with green salad," said the waiter. "For desert, we have rose petal ice cream."

"Rose petal ice cream?" I asked Mother.

I had heard of rose petal preserves, but not ice cream. Chocolate ice cream would have sounded so much better.

Within minutes, the smell of piping hot soup reached my nose. Served in a gold-rimmed, white china bowl was a mixture of cubed carrots, potatoes, parsnips, onions, and perfectly rounded matzo balls dancing in beef broth, sprinkled parsley, and snow white sour cream.

"This is delicious, Mama," I said, tasting it. After not having eaten for the entire day, the soup warmed my tummy and reminded me of home. We had barely finished when the waiter came back and placed before us the largest Wiener schnitzel I had ever seen in my life. On top of a mount of mashed potatoes lay an enormous piece of tenderized, breaded veal, the size of four large hands.

"Mama, this is huge!"

"Eat as much as you can, Sperantza. We'll take the rest to the room in case you get hungry later on."

I didn't eat desert that evening. I much preferred smelling roses rather than eating them.

The following morning, rested and refreshed, we got ready for another day in Sofia. After breakfast, we got back on the bus heading for the city center.

"In a few minutes, we'll be arriving downtown where we will walk to the famous Red Square," said the tour guide. "Afterward, we'll have lunch and then get back on the road. We're expecting to reach the Turkish border by morning." Just as she finished, the coach pulled into a parking lot where a sea of buses were all neatly lined up next to each other. The bus driver turned off the music, stopped the bus, and opened the front doors. Row by row, we were dismissed. There was a somber feeling in the air as we stepped down onto the dark, gray, cobblestone plaza. A myriad of little squares shaped in a small circle opened up into successively larger circles, forming this austere-looking Red Square Plaza.

Placing my feet on one of those squares, I looked down at my red sandals and was reminded of the blood shed by those soldiers who fought for what they believed was freedom. But they died in vain because none of us were really free, not under such a regime.

As I pondered how many others felt like I did, my thoughts were interrupted by the sound of a camera click. As I raised my head, a telephoto lens held by a man with dark sunglasses was pointed toward me from several meters away.

I felt Mother's hand grab and squeeze mine. Immediately, I turned towards the tour guide who was in the middle of her Marxist ideology discourse.

"They died believing in something greater than themselves. They died for Communism, a system where we're all equal, where there are no rich or poor, where we all live in a state of communal benefit in want of nothing, in peace and harmony."

"Did she really believe what she was saying?" I thought. Communist theory sounded, perhaps, like utopia; but, in reality, it was a disaster. Communism was failing, and failing miserably. The rich got richer. The poor got poorer. Those who stood for the right were silenced. Those who spoke for freedom were captured behind walls and held behind iron curtains. Many who believed in God were persecuted, tortured, and killed. Many of those who didn't believe turned into the murderers and torturers who snuffed out their spirit.

Those who led, did so by corruption, hatred, and greed. Bribery was their way of life. They were committed to keeping their positions for their

SPERANTZA ADRIANA PASOS

own benefit. People had no motivation to do anything else but accept the miserable form of government that led and abused the country. And Bulgaria seemed to be no different.

I don't know what kind of expression I must have had on my face, but when I heard the click of the camera trigger and saw the lens pointed in my direction once again, it dawned on me this man wasn't taking pictures for his family album. I had to be on guard. I forced a smile on my face and then turned slowly around, so that my back would face him. I continued hearing the camera go off until the tour guide, Mrs. Ionescu, finished her speech and we finally headed for another location.

Chapter 11

After lunch, we boarded our coach and settled back into the comfortable, oversized red-velour chairs with crisp, white head rests for the ride to Turkey. Toward the evening, Mother pulled out her Turkish dictionary and began writing something in her tiny notebook, the size of a playing card. I leaned over, and what I saw sent shivers up my spine: "Help! We want to escape! We want Political Asylum. Where can we go? Can you help? Where is the Austrian Embassy?"

I cringed thinking what would happen if anyone saw what Mother was doing. Although seated by the window, somewhat protected from those across the aisle from us, she still risked being seen by those behind us, not to mention the tour guide who constantly walked up and down the aisle.

From the corner of my eye, I looked nervously to see if someone, anyone, was watching us. Mother crouched down as much as she could into the chair. Since it was getting dark outside, she continued.

Looking up a few words in the dictionary, she would write them down, then slowly and methodically rip the page out of her notebook and hide it in her purse. Then, she'd begin the process all over again.

I must have fallen asleep because when I woke up, the bus had stopped. "What time is it, Mama?" I asked.

"It's almost 6 o'clock in the morning."

"Where are we?"

"At the Turkish border, honey."

"Why are we stopped?"

"I don't know, Sperantza. We've been here for several hours now, but I'm sure they'll tell us soon."

Just then, Mrs. Ionescu walked onto the bus, turned on the microphone, and made the following announcement: "Bună Dimineața, Romanian citizens. We have arrived at the Turkish border, but we have some problems. The officials refuse to let us in the country because we have no passports."

"We have no passports?" I asked, shocked.

"We have what we call a common passport," said the tour guide, "but they say that's not enough."

"What's that?" I thought.

"A common passport," Mrs. Ionescu continued, "is a list of all passengers and their pertinent information. That's all they really need, but the Turks won't accept it. They told us that, without individual passports, we'll have to go back home. We'll try one more time to see what we can do, but...." She glanced back outside. "The way it looks right now," she said, shaking her head, "we're not getting in."

As she spoke, I remembered what Dad had said about our passports, how the police held them, and how we were only allowed to have them when traveling abroad. Here we were, abroad, without our passports. It finally dawned on me. No one had given them to us. I just assumed the tour guide had them. I realized we had been denied even the most basic recognizable travel document in the world—a passport. That was unbelievable. It meant we had left Romania, entered and traveled through Bulgaria, and now stood at the border of Turkey, wanting to enter yet another foreign country, all without any international identity whatsoever, except a piece of paper. It was unheard of.

I looked at Mother. She just closed her eyes, praying, no doubt. As my gaze moved beyond her face, onto the horizon, I caught a glimpse of a most glorious sight. The sun was rising into the cloudless sky, bathing the deep blue Marmara Sea in thick streaks of gold with reflections touching the soft waves. Together, they began what looked like a most beautiful dance, holding each other in a soft embrace until another ray came in to join this incredible show of light, water, and movement.

Yachts neatly docked beside the unspeakably beautiful villas lined up against the shore. Framed by luscious green trees and manicured lawns, these homes painted in hues of gold, beige, and burnt sienna appeared as sentinels on guard against the immenseness of the sea.

Watching this beautiful palette of color and imagery unfold just outside my window, I couldn't help but wonder what it must feel like to be free—free to live, free to think, free to worship...

Oh, Freedom! Why are you ever so elusive? I can see you, but cannot have you. I can feel you, but cannot hold you. I can sense you, but cannot touch you. Oh, Freedom! What does it cost to attain you? What is your price? How can I be so near to you, yet still so far? I must go back now, but wonder how long till I see you again? And when will I ever be free?

Tears began flooding my eyes. "You mustn't cry, Sperantza," I kept saying to myself. "As hard as this may be, you mustn't cry. You mustn't cry." Finishing my internal monologue, I closed my eyes. "Oh, Freedom, do I have to let you go?"

My heart ached. I could see that country, that land, that sea, and those people. They were free. I was not. Confined to a motor coach and held by invisible shackles, I was a prisoner of a twisted, sick regime.

Feeling as though freedom was slipping through my very fingers, the only thing I could hold onto was hope.... Hope for maybe another time...

"What does this mean? What will we do now? What about the money we paid?" The passengers asked question after question. People began to get anxious as they wondered what would happen next. I already knew. It was clear. I couldn't understand why they even asked. It was obvious that we were going back.

When Mrs. Ionescu came back in the bus, I was ready for her announcement. "The Turkish Government has no means of verifying our identity based on our list of passengers. The document we have is not considered official. Because of international laws, they said, all passengers must hold individual passports in order to be allowed entry into their country." There was a big sigh of disappointment from all the passengers.

I knew it. "Mama, we're going back," I whispered in panic.

"Shh," she motioned. "The guide is still speaking."

"But, after going through what seemed like an interminable lesson in law," Mrs. Ionescu continued, "the border officials said they'll make an exception for us just this once. So, we have their approval to enter Turkey."

"What? We do?" I could hardly believe my ears. Moments before, I felt all hope was gone. Now, a flicker was slowly returning.

"There is one condition, however," the guide said. "We must stay together as a group at all times. We cannot separate."

I felt my head spin. My spectrum of emotions went from hope to despair to hope and crashing back down to despair, all within minutes. "How in the world will we ever escape," I thought, "if we must stay together?"

Chapter 12

I t was early afternoon when we arrived at the hotel. Located on a busy street in Istanbul, Hotel Kavac was modern and beautiful. We stepped out of our motor coach and into the lobby with floors covered by Turkish rugs displaying an intricate tapestry of colors and motifs. The rich reds, browns, yellows, greens, and blues pleasantly greeted our eyes. As we sat down and waited for our assigned rooms, we overheard our tour guide saying:

"The hotel is overbooked. There is a shortage of rooms. It appears we will have to double up in order to fit."

At just about that time, Mrs. Dinescu, a lovely elderly doctor from Breaza, approached Mother.

"Oh, Mrs. Totpal, I've just heard they'll be placing us in a room together. I told the tour guide I wanted to room with you and your daughter. We will go shopping together, it will just be lovely."

I couldn't believe my ears.

"That's wonderful," Mother said, pleasantly.

"Wonderful?" I thought. "How can Mother think this is wonderful?

How in the world will we be able to talk, to plan, to figure out our escape?" I couldn't see how this was going to work.

The small, crowded lobby made me feel claustrophobic. Tourists constantly entered and exited through the revolving door. Some were sitting, others were standing. The strong smell of smoke made me choke, and the sounds of the Turkish language felt so foreign. My senses were becoming overloaded with all the commotion around me.

For as long as I could remember, I had been exposed to foreign languages. Growing up, I remember looking forward to hearing the weather reports because they were given in several languages: Italian, French, Russian, Hungarian, Bulgarian. I loved the sounds of new words. Furthermore, my grandmother, who was fluent in French, taught me how to speak it beginning at the tender age of five. When I started school, I continued learning it along with a bit of German and Latin. But Turkish was so different. I couldn't make out one single word.

Seated there, waiting, I felt fear creep in once again. "How will we ever communicate with these people? How will we make ourselves understood? How will we understand them? How will we get away? How will we escape?" I thought.

My thoughts were suddenly interrupted by Mother's words. "Come on Sperantza, they've assigned us our room."

"Wait. What about Mrs. Dinescu?" I asked.

"Mrs. Dinescu will have her own room," Mother replied, walking quickly towards the elevator.

"But, I thought ...."

"Sperantza!" she said sternly.

I quietly followed her into the lift where an attendant pressed the 4th floor button. As I stepped in, I felt I had entered a room not an elevator, it seemed so spacious to me. Accustomed to the ones in Romania that were narrow, dark, and small, with barely enough room to carry four people standing like sardines next to each other, never mind their luggage— (because if you had luggage, it would mean several trips back and forth;

unless of course, there was an electricity shortage to stop you mid-way until the power came back which sometimes would take hours)—this, in comparison, was luxurious.

When the elevator stopped at the 4th floor, the attendant motioned us to follow him. We turned right into the semi-dark hallway, then right again. Five doors to the left, we stopped in front of Room 405. With the large key, hanging from his neck, the attendant opened the door and we stepped inside.

Although the room was small, the afternoon sun filled it with soft light, creating a spacious, airy feeling. The windows were opened, and a soft breeze blew the transparent, gauze-like curtains. I could hear voices coming from outside. As I got closer to the window, I saw our room faced the inner courtyard. And then, I heard the door close.

"It must have been the attendant," I said. Hearing no reply, I turned around only to see Mother's pensive gaze transfixed upon that window.

There was no need for words since, in that silence, volumes were spoken...

We both just stood there, gazing through yet another window of our life.

Chapter 13

Time flew and we were soon awakened from our reverie by a knock at the door. "Mrs. Totpal, Mrs. Totpal, are you coming?" It was Mrs. Dinescu. "Come on, let's go," she said, as Mother opened the door. "They're letting us go explore on our own for about an hour until dinner," she said, excitedly. "We must stay within ten minutes of the hotel at all times, but there are lots of shops nearby."

Closing the door behind us, we followed her toward the elevator, and nearly tripped over a man seated in an armchair.

"How can he read that newspaper with those sunglasses on?" I thought. "It's so dark in here." I didn't think much of it since the lift arrived, and we went downstairs.

Stepping outside onto the sidewalk was electrifying. Twelve lanes of traffic zoomed by constantly. Cars and tramways, buses and vans, minibuses and taxis, horns beeping, sirens screeching, along with the sounds of whistling ships in the harbor made my head spin.

Mother held my hand tightly as we squeezed by the multitudes on the narrow sidewalks. They were mostly olive-skinned men dressed in suits.

Others sat on three-short-legged wooden stools sipping what looked like a yellow drink from tiny glass containers and puffing smoke from what looked like a very strange contraption.

Every now and then we'd pass by a few women wearing what looked like long beige overcoats and tight scarves on their heads that wrapped around their faces and covered them up to their eyes. This was, indeed, a metropolis, the likes of which I had only read about.

Further up the street, on the opposite side, some women stood in what looked like very large windows. "They seem so friendly, Mama. Why are they standing in those windows?" I naively asked.

"I'll explain later. Just keep walking."

"I see," I said, still not comprehending exactly why.

As we turned the corner, we entered a small shop that sold trinkets and souvenirs. Stepping onto the elegant marble floor, we looked around. Displayed on large swivels were large, colorful, postcards of Istanbul. I reached for one and pulled it out, only to find that it unraveled like an accordion. Scared, I tried to put it back.

The shopkeeper, who I assume had heard us speak Romanian as we entered, came over and kindly said: "Nu vă faceți probleme." Don't worry. There is no problem. "I'll put it back."

I realized then how careful we still had to be. This man surprised us by speaking our own language. I wondered how many others understood everything we said. Before we knew it, it was dinner time so we headed back to the hotel.

After our evening meal, we returned back to our room. Strangely enough, the man I had seen when we left was still there, still holding his paper, still wearing his dark sunglasses. "He must be a slow reader," I thought...

Back in our room, I threw myself down on the bed, exhausted. Closing the window, Mother motioned me towards the bathroom. Then, in a loud voice, she said: "Come Sperantza, I'll prepare the bath for you."

"Yes, that would be wonderful, Mama," I responded just as loud, following her lead. She turned on the lights, turned on the water, and closed the door.

"Now, listen," she said, in a low voice, "this room is safer. They can't hear us in here. And with the water running, we have some background noise. When we talk about our plan, we'll do it in here." And as if she had read my mind, she whispered, "Sperantza, you know that man outside our room wearing dark glasses?"

"Yes, I wondered about him. He's been there since we left. What is he doing?"

"I can tell you one thing. He is not reading the newspaper. He is watching us."

"Watching us?" I said, my eyes growing bigger.

"Sperantza," Mama continued, "I don't want to alarm you, but we are being watched everywhere. He is not the only one, either, darling."

"He's not? What do you mean?"

"When we left our room this afternoon, and I grabbed your hand just before you almost stumbled over him, my eyes caught a glimpse of several others down the corridor. Spaced out between doors, all wearing dark glasses and newspapers in hand, these are no visitors in this hotel. That's why we must be so careful," she continued in a hushed voice. "We are constantly being watched, even though in a free country. Be careful what you say! Even in here. We must look normal, act normal, talk normal, so as to raise no suspicion."

"Tomorrow morning," she continued, "we are scheduled to visit the Topkapi Palace. After lunch, they're thinking of taking us to the Bazaar. That's when we'll try to make our escape. I don't know how we'll do it since we've been told we must stay together at all times, but we must try."

I felt so overwhelmed, so scared. How in the world would we get away? When and where would we go? How would we manage?

Sensing my anxiety, Mother said, "Sperantza, do not worry. God will make a way!" When she began to pray, I felt peace flood my soul again, even though kneeling down on that hard marble floor.

"Father, we thank you for bringing us here safely. Please be with our dear ones back home, and give us peace. Help us, protect us and give us wisdom for tomorrow. Please show us where to go and what to do. In Your sweet name we pray, Amen."

Chapter 14

As we left our room the following morning, I saw the other men Mother had told me about. She was right. They all wore dark glasses and all held newspapers in their hands.

After a delicious breakfast at the restaurant, the tour guide announced the itinerary for the day.

"We will be visiting the famous Topkapi Palace this morning and, after lunch, on to the largest shopping place in the world—The Grand Bazaar."

Home to all the Ottoman sultans for a period of nearly four centuries, the palace was a sight to behold. Several courtyards led into the fabulous interior where our eyes were delighted by the magnificent treasury rooms containing art works from the Islamic world dating back to the 13th century all the way up through to the 20th. From the famed Topkapi dagger, the inspiration for the world-renowned movie, *Topkapi*, to the pride of the Topkapi Palace Museum and its most valuable single exhibit, the Spoonmaker's Diamond, this was something I had never experienced.

The Topkapi Dagger was 35 centimeters long. On one side of the sheath were three large, clear emeralds the size of pigeon's eggs surrounded with diamonds. It is for that reason it had become famous as the "Emerald Dagger." The sheath, made of gold, showed a separate beauty and richness of its own. The enameled flowers and diamonds constituted a separate motif that dazzled the eyes. At the lightly turned end of the sheath, I noticed another large emerald.

"The Spoonmaker's Diamond," said the tour guide, "is the pride of Topkapi's Palace Museum and its most valuable single exhibit."

An 86-carat pear-shaped diamond, it was surrounded by a double-row of forty-nine old mine-cut diamonds, which gave it the appearance of a full moon lighting a bright and shining sky amidst the stars.

Leaving those incredible sights, I began feeling butterflies in my stomach knowing that the hour of our escape was nearing.

"After lunch," said the tour guide, "take advantage and relax a little in your rooms until three o'clock when we will be heading to the Bazaar. Tomorrow, we will be sightseeing on the Bosporus. Then, in the afternoon, we'll be returning home."

Back in our room, I felt my stomach cramp again. "Mama, I feel like throwing up. I'm so scared! What if they catch us? What if Mrs. Dinescu wants to come with us? How will we get away? What if someone sees us? And if we do escape, what if they come looking for us? They have one more day here, you know."

"Sperantza, all I know is that we must pray. And we must trust. God will take care of us just as He promised."

Mother always knew how to calm my fears. Laying in bed close to her, feeling her arms around me, and hearing the sounds of the clock softly ticking, tick, tock, tick, tock, finally lulled me to sleep. But not for long.

"It's time to go, Sperantza," said Mother gently shaking me. "It's almost 3:00 o'clock."

"I'm coming," I said, still half asleep. Hurriedly, we made our way to the lobby only to find out that we were the first ones there.

"Right this way," said a tall gentleman in Romanian, pointing us to the restaurant where the tour guide was seated at the table, waiting.

I felt my knees begin to shake and thought, "Oh, no, do they know of our plan? Did they hear us talk in our room? Why are we the only ones here? Why just the tour guide? Where is everyone else?"

"Come, sit," Mrs. Ionescu said, inviting us to her table. "We've been waiting for you. Apparently, the food at lunch hasn't settled well with many of our passengers. They are quite ill with what could be a stomach virus. So, we have no choice, but to postpone our trip to the Bazaar until tomorrow. By then, I hope they'll all be better."

"Oh, thank God," I thought, breathing a sigh of relief.

"Why is your daughter so pale, Mrs. Totpal?" the tour guide asked, as she looked at me with concerned eyes. "I hope she's not getting sick too."

"I think she's just tired," replied Mother. "This schedule has been quite intense for her."

"Well, take care of yourself. Go back to your room and rest. Tomorrow, you'll be doing a lot of walking. The Bazaar is immense!"

That evening, the tour guide asked if she could join us for dinner.

"Yes, please do," said Mother. This was strange. She had never sat with us before. I was suspicious, wondering why our table. Had she overheard any of our conversations? Or, had the men, or should I say, spies-in-black, overheard anything we said from outside the room? Did they sense our fears or read it in our faces?

Thoughts kept rushing through my head. I chose to stay quiet instead. "Oh, God, help me not to say something stupid," I prayed.

Amidst the small talk, the food finally arrived. "This smells wonderful," Mother said. The aroma of delicious bread filled the room. Olives, wonderful, fat, and juicy green, black olives, feta cheese, and a large bowl of dipping oil with fresh seasonings made for a delightful appetizer. Course after course, the food was a display of freshness, vivid colors, and incredible taste.

"I don't think I can possibly handle desert," Mother sighed. But who can resist such temptation? A decadent sweet pastry, cut the size of a match box—this was the original Turkish baklava—made out of delicious walnuts drenched in honey and wrapped between layers and layers of Phyllo dough.

It was during that indulging moment that Mrs. Ionescu, our tour guide, said, "Mrs. Totpal, I tell you, this is the best tour I've led in many years. I know no one will remain behind."

Under the table, I felt mother's foot press against mine. I understood I must be careful.

"You know," she continued, "on my previous tour, I had a gentleman who seemed so pleasant. I never thought he would defect. He even paid for a day cruise on the Bosporus for all of us. I couldn't believe it when we never saw him again. He must have escaped during the Bazaar trip."

"Hmm," I heard Mother say, her face revealing no emotion. I felt blood rushing to my face, but prayed God would help me keep my composure.

"I just couldn't believe it," she said, hitting her hand on the table for emphasis. "He was the last person I could have imagined to do such a thing. But anyway, that's why I'm so happy with this group. I know that nobody will defect this time."

I was relieved when that conversation ended and couldn't wait to get back to the room. In the "security" of our small bathroom, I finally asked.

"Mother, why did she tell us those things? Do you think that she knows? This is so frightening."

"I don't believe she knows. But we must be careful—careful with our words and actions. The only way we can possibly do it, is by God's strength. We must trust Him. We must focus on Him. He has made a way so far and will continue to do so. Don't be afraid! God is with us! Look how the itinerary was changed. Do you think that was simply a coincidence?"

"Think about it," Mother continued. "After the Bazaar, the bus is scheduled to leave for Romania. That works to our advantage. Should we have gone to the Bazaar today as planned, they would have had one more day in Turkey to look for us."

"Tomorrow, we must be ready to shop, like everyone else. We'll take this bag with us," she said, pointing to a medium size orange duffle bag. We'll carry the camera in there, too. But remember the Deutsch Marks. Don't leave it out of sight!"

"What about our clothes, our shoes, the things we need?"

"Sweetheart, we can't take anything with us. Imagine what would happen if they would check our bags and discover our clothes inside?"

"Then wha... wha... what will I wear the next day, and the next?"

"My child, the only thing I know right now is that, somehow, our God will provide."

"Do you even know where we're going?"

"My plan is to grab a taxi to the Austrian Embassy. Once there, we'll request to be sent to Austria, to join Auntie Lia and Uncle Nicu."

The fact that Mother had a plan eased my anxiety a bit. "The only thing we had to do," I thought, "was to get away—away from all those people, with no one suspecting anything, keep a poker face at all times, make our way out of the Bazaar, find a taxi, communicate with the driver in a language we didn't know, and then find the Austrian Embassy."

"It's easy... It's easy... It's easy," I kept repeating over and over again in my head. Although my words were positive, my stomach didn't seem to get the same message. It tossed and turned into knots as my hands and feet began to shake once again.

"Come, my child," said Mother, "we must get to bed." Kneeling beside me, she began to pray: "Father, You are our God. Our only security, the only One we trust. Our hearts are heavy and our souls are anxious tonight. We need Your rest, Your presence and Your peace. You promised to protect us. You promised to direct us. We have no other help, but You. Don't leave us, please. Comfort us with your presence and your love, and give us the strength we need to face tomorrow. And lead us to freedom, I pray in Jesus' name. Amen."

"Amen." I said, softly, suddenly feeling peace again. "I love you, Mama," I whispered.

I felt her arms envelop me. Kissing my forehead, she began singing a lullaby that transported me back home to Daddy and my little sister. Fighting back the tears, I closed my eyes and, at last, fell into a restless sleep.

Chapter 15

The morning came faster than I had hoped. We gathered all our belongings and took them to the lobby. Mrs. Dinescu, as vivacious as ever, waved and said, "Mrs. Totpal, Mrs. Totpal, let's stay together."

"Oh, my," I thought. How is this ever going to work? The tour guide gave us the last instructions before we separated as a group into the Bazaar.

"Now, you must keep together in small groups. That way you can find your way back," she said.

"Let's see, it's eight o'clock. The Bazaar is an underground labyrinth with many gates that lead to other parts of Istanbul. Remember the name of the gate we are entering because that is the gate through which you will have to come back. We will meet back at the hotel at 1:00 p.m. Remember this location. In case you are late, we will wait an additional 30 minutes. After that, we will depart. Be here on time. Also, be careful with your belongings. Stay together in small groups and have an enjoyable time. See you back in five hours."

"Let's go Mrs. Totpal," said Mrs. Ionescu, excitedly.

"What are you interested in purchasing Mrs. Ionescu," asked Mother.

"I'm looking for leather goods, specifically a leather jacket."

"There is a leather store right across the street," continued Mother. "Let's go in."

I couldn't believe it. Mother was inviting her to go with us. "How will we ever separate from her?" I wondered.

Once inside, I saw many members of our group mesmerized by such fine workmanship. I had never seen so many leather jackets in one store. I walked ever so carefully, not even daring to touch them. Short and knee-length jackets came in a multitude of colors. Long coats in rich reddish browns, deep forest greens and midnight blues lined up against the wall, and ahh, the smell of leather. Mother watched Mrs. Ionescu, who had apparently fallen in love with a butter-pecan leather coat.

"I must try this on," she said, smiling to the shopkeeper.

"Come in, come in," I heard him say invitingly to her in his broken Romanian.

As she disappeared behind the long, gray fabric curtain, I felt mother's hand grab mine. "Let's go," she said, in a low voice. We left the store and dashed across the busy street, heading toward the Bazaar. In front of the entrance were hundreds of black and white taxis waiting for passengers. To the right was a massive gate. Several stairs led down to one of the many entrances to this underground city. As we entered the Bazaar, it was magical. I felt as if I had stepped into a page right out of Ali Baba and *The Thousand and One Nights.*

It was another world. Lights lit up the otherwise dark place. Oriental music played in the background. Shopkeepers with olive-skinned faces smiled and stared intently at me as I passed by, their snow white teeth peeking from underneath large ebony mustaches. They spoke in languages I couldn't understand and motioned us to come in.

All this commotion and sounds felt exhilarating, yet scary—music playing, merchants selling, bargaining and showing off their goods. Some followed us and grabbed us by the hand to lead us in their stores. Others placed their goods into our hands, not wanting to accept no for an answer, and almost forcing us to buy.

Large reels of gold of all sorts shone and sparkled—weaved gold, thin gold, intricately-designed gold. Never in my life had I seen so much gold in one single place. There was sparkling jewelry, clothes, shoes and leather purses. And of course, there were those famous Turkish rugs weaved out of a kaleidoscope of colors. From deep hues of crimson to intensely rich blues—from beige-browns to almond toast—some soft and others coarse, they seemed to cover the walls and the floors. Many were piled up high on the sidewalks, waiting for that eager customer. Breathtaking! Absolutely breathtaking! That was the feeling that I had.

"We need some sandals for you," said Mother, rather loudly.

"We do?" I asked, naively. I didn't feel comfortable going in any of those shops. Just as she said those words, I heard familiar sounds. As I turned around, I saw several individuals from our group pass us by. I smiled, nervously. They smiled back.

"Yes, yes, we must buy some sandals," she continued in the same high voice. "Let's look in this shop." As we entered, I realized more people from our group were walking past us.

"Isn't this amazing?" they said as they walked by. We forced another smile again.

"Let's keep our eyes on the rest of them," Mother said. "We'll go down a few shops. Once we're assured that all of them have entered the Bazaar, we'll make our way back to the exit and grab a taxi. At least we will have something in our hands."

"Mama, I'm uncomfortable with all these men staring at us. Do you see them? They're all staring."

"Listen," she said. "We're tourists and they're trying to make a living. Don't be afraid."

"But, can't we find a store where a lady can help us?"

"Well, I haven't seen any so far, but we can look for one."

We walked and walked but realized the only women we saw were the ones doing the shopping. Some were covered up with long jackets—some gray, some black—and their heads were covered up as well. The only adornment I saw was the gold bracelets on their sleeves. What shocked me was how many they wore. It wasn't one or two or three. These women wore them from their wrists to their shoulders on both hands. I later found out that was a symbol of their husbands' love for them. The amount of bracelets they displayed was apparently in direct proportion to the amount of love their husbands had for them.

We finally entered a shop. Dictionary in hand, Mother tried communicating with the shopkeeper. He finally understood what we wanted and measured my foot. After several tries, we found a burgundy platform shoe that fit just right. Paying for it, we walked out, with sandals in hand.

"Wait!" trumpeted Mother.

"What's wrong?"

"Quick! Get in," she said, as she pushed me into another shop. "I saw some people from our group." Just as we thought we were safe to turn around, we saw our tour guide come towards us.

"Mrs. Totpal, you're going the wrong way," she said.

I felt as though I had just stepped in freshly poured coal tar pitch. I couldn't move. To my relief I heard Mother respond.

"We're just looking at these incredible shops. Look at these sandals, I just purchased for my daughter. A bargain! Aren't they great?"

I was shaking like a reed inside.

"Those are beautiful. Where did you get them?" asked Mrs. Ionescu.

"From a shop further up," Mother responded, giving her detailed directions.

"Well, we'll see you in a couple of hours," she said, heading towards the center shops.

"Whew! That was scary," I whispered.

"I know," Mother said, closing her eyes for a moment and breathing a sigh of relief. "But God is with us and He'll give us strength. Don't you forget that, Sperantza."

"Let's look in here," she said, pulling me yet into another shop. "We'll wait inside a while until Mrs. Ionescu is out of sight."

"I know, but what if we run into someone else from our group as we head out?"

"We have no choice, my child. We'll have to run the risk and do it," said Mother. "We've been in here for about an hour, and we've seen lots of them pass by. I even saw Mrs. Dinescu a little while ago. She was walking together with several families. Thank God she didn't see us."

Stepping outside the shop into the main avenue, we continued our way back to the exit gate. But with every step I took, I felt my feet get heavier and heavier. I couldn't help but wonder what would happen if we would run into someone we knew again. What would we say? Where were we going?

In the distance, I could see daylight peeking through the main gate of the Bazaar.

"We are not far," I thought. "Not far, just a few more meters. Just a few more meters," I kept telling myself. But my feet would not carry me.

"Mother, I can't walk. I can't anymore."

"You must walk. You must walk and be brave. Look we're almost there. You can't let fear cripple you, Sperantza. Come on, let's go. We can't give up now." Grabbing my hand, she started pulling me behind her as she would a rag doll. "We mustn't give up," she'd say, "we're almost there, almost there, almost there."

The light was getting brighter and brighter. I could even see the stairs leading up to the outside plaza. But with every step I took, I felt as though I was on a merry-go-round. Question after question rushed into my head, bouncing back and forth without an answer. "What will we do? Where will we go? What if someone we know sees us? What will we say? What then? What next?"

I breathed a silent prayer. "Jesus, please help us. We're almost to the taxi plaza. Don't let us run into someone we know. Protect us, please."

We finally reached the stairs. Anywhere else in the Bazaar, we could possibly camouflage ourselves by entering into a store. But what possible explanation could we give if we were seen leaving the Bazaar at such an early hour?

Mother and I looked at each other. We both hesitated, a bit. We both knew this was one of the most dangerous moments we were facing so far. She took a deep breath and then stepped ahead of me to climb up the stairs. I followed.

Within moments we were outside staring at what looked like a sea of taxis. Mother walked over to one and showed the driver a little piece of paper then dashed into the back seat. I followed.

As the driver pulled away from the plaza, a wave of emotion came over me. I couldn't believe it. We were on our way to the Austrian Embassy, soon to be reunited with my aunt and uncle. We had made it! We were free!

Chapter 16

Even though I should have felt much more secure in the confines of that taxi, my head continued to be bombarded with question after question. "Why is he taking so long? Why hasn't he found the place yet? Why are we going in circles? Is he trying to find the Austrian Embassy or is he driving us around just to take our money?"

"Mama, we've passed by this building several times, now," I said, frustrated. "He's just going around and around. Is he lost? He keeps looking at the paper you gave him. How can we ask him?"

"We can't. We'll have to trust that God will help him find the place," Mother said.

Sitting close to Mother in that taxi was the only thing that reassured me. Here we were in a foreign country, in the metropolis of Istanbul. We did not speak the language; we did not know where we were going and we were at the mercy of a taxi driver who seemed as lost as I felt.

Finally, he stopped the car. He then got out and pointed us toward a small side street that led behind the building we had circled so many times.

"Austria Embassy, Austria Embassy," he said in broken English.

Mother paid him the fare, and we headed in that direction. Not far from where we had been dropped off stood a large, gray two-story building. A square plaque next to the entrance held several lines written in Turkish. Underneath the fourth line we saw the words, Austrian Embassy.

"Thank God!" I said.

"Quick. Let's go in," said Mother.

We climbed up the stairs to the second floor and entered the embassy with such expectancy and desire. I felt this was the answer to our quest; the place that would put an end to the fears of our journey and the way to reunite us with our family.

"May I help you?" asked the young lady behind the counter.

"We would like to see the Honorable Consul, please," I managed in broken German.

"Do you have an audience?"

"No."

"I'm sorry, he's not available," came the response. "Can I help you?"

"My mother and I are from Romania," I continued. "We request Political Asylum. My aunt and uncle are already in Austria and we want to join them."

With an expression that denoted she must have understood my naiveté, she responded: "I'm sorry. You cannot go to Austria. You must stay in Turkey."

She continued, "The immigration laws state you must remain in the first democratic...." I couldn't even hear, much less understand what she was saying.

I must have had a blank look on my face.

"What is she saying?" asked Mother.

"She can't help us," I responded.

"Why not?"

"Mama, I don't understand why not," I said frustrated, feeling as though someone had grabbed me by my throat. "I don't know what she said. I don't understand her. She said something about the laws or immigration rules."

78

As the woman behind the counter turned around and left the room, I felt as though my hopes vanished along with her. I stared at the door that had just closed behind her, hoping and wishing she would come back with maybe another answer. After several minutes, it dawned on me that she would not.

So, we just stood there, Mother and I. Shocked. Dumbfounded. Trying to process all the information and accept the fact that we were back to square one was heart-wrenching.

The plan hadn't worked and it wasn't as if we had other options. This wasn't plan A of A, B or C. It was the only plan we had. The only one we had considered, and it had failed.

As we left the Austrian Embassy with my hopes shattered and feeling completely confused, I wondered, "What next?"

Back on the street, I felt the warmth of my mother's hand as she gently touched mine. "Sperantza, God is still God. He will help us. I don't know how. I don't know when. But what I do know is what He has promised— that He won't leave us. Do you understand?"

As hard as I tried, my mouth could utter no response. Mother's words always soothed me in the past. Her demeanor was always one of strength and assurance. Without a doubt, she drew her courage and faith from the One who was much greater than any circumstance. But, at this very moment, I felt lost and wondered how in the world she could still see a way out of the mess we were in. How could she still believe that? Had she not heard? Had she not seen what had just happened?

My thoughts raced. "We're on the streets of Istanbul, in the middle of Turkey, a Muslim country. We don't speak their language. We don't understand a word they're saying. We have nowhere to go and no one to help us, and Mother still says God will help! How? How can He possibly help? I feel lost, so totally lost in this huge place. Worst of all, I feel nobody knows. Worst yet, nobody even cares."

Walking down the busy street, Mother and I found a place to sit. It was a concrete ledge, the bottom part of an otherwise black wrought iron fence that encircled a large building. Leaning against the fence in complete silence, we watched person after person and car after car pass us by for I don't even know how long.

"Maybe our bus will drive by this way," I heard Mother finally say. "It's past 1:30 PM, you know?"

"What would we tell them, if they did?" I asked, almost carelessly.

Pondering upon Mother's comment, I wondered if that was our only way out—going back to the hell we had just come out of, days earlier. I felt as though for a moment, she, too, saw no way out! As a mother today, I can't even begin to imagine what it must have felt like to face such danger not only for her, but also for her child.

Mother later told me she had heard that Turks deported people who tried to immigrate; that the police would walk the streets and identify random people, requesting proof of identification. If they had none, they would incarcerate them until such documents could be produced or their identity be proven.

Understanding our situation, Mother was literally waiting for someone to pick us up off the streets. After several hours when no one did, she realized the only way out, barring a miracle, was to return home.

Not knowing what she knew, I felt a surge of hope rise within me when, across the street, I saw a man dressed in blue uniform with gold buttons, and a blue cap.

"Mother, let's cross," I said to her, jumping up and pulling her into the middle of the street. Before she even realized what was happening, we were already on the other side.

"Bonjour, Monsieur! Je voudrais l'asile politique."

He smiled kindly and motioned us to follow him into an office building not too far from where we had been sitting. It was a police station. Several men in uniforms looked at us as we entered. He spoke to them in Turkish and one asked, "Do you speak English?"

I shook my head "no" and said, "Je parle Français."

"Sprechen sie Deutsch?"

"Ein Bichen," I responded. Very little.

I could see they were in a quandary. They couldn't understand what we were saying, and we couldn't understand them. The men spoke some more and then two of them motioned for us to follow. Leading us outside the police station, they took us across the street into what looked like a restaurant. The place we entered was very dark. Once inside, the policemen approached a lady who came walking towards us.

"Bonjour, Mesdames. Je parle Français. Comment est-ce que je peux vous aider?"

I couldn't believe my ears. She spoke French! Finally, I could communicate with someone who would understand me.

"Nous sommes de Roumanie, içi on visite et nous ne voulons pas returner a Roumanie. Nous besoin d'asile politique. A cause religieuse." We are here in an excursion from Romania and we want Political Asylum because of religious persecution.

She translated what we said, and then she turned toward us and added, "The policemen said this is a small station, which has no authority to take you in. You will need to go the Grand Police Station. They can help you there."

"How much will it cost," Mother asked?

"You won't have to pay anything. It's all taken care of."

"Merçi beaucoup, merçi Madame," I said to her.

Walking out of that place, we followed the policemen who crossed the street and motioned us to get into the taxi that was parked in front of the station. One of the officers spoke to the driver, who nodded and took off, driving us to yet another location.

When he pulled into the Grand Police Station, it seemed as though the parking lot was filled with police cars. The taxi stopped and the driver got out of the car, motioning us to follow him.

Entering a large office, we saw a man in civilian clothes seated in a dark chair behind a silver gray metal desk. The taxi driver spoke to him as he motioned for us to sit in the nearby seats.

After the driver left, two more men came in. They all spoke Turkish and stared at us intently. Not understanding a word they said made me feel even more uncomfortable. As they talked, they would walk behind us and then stop. After a few minutes, they would walk in front of us and then stop again; then beside us and stop again. All along, their penetrating gazes made me feel as though they were burning holes through my flesh.

Feeling looked upon from every direction as some sort of merchandise placed on a market piazza, I tried hard to hold back my tears—especially when, after a while, they would say something again and then start laughing. Throughout the conversation, it seemed, Mother understood one word, but it was the word she feared the most—harem. I felt so helpless. After about an hour, one said:

"Sprechen sie Deutsch?"

"Nein," I answered.

"Do you speak English?"

"No. Je parle Francais," I said.

"Identity? Papieren?"

We had none. We had no identity. We had no papers, no passports, nothing to prove who we were.

They began making phone call after phone call. The tall man behind the desk smiled at us while the rest stared. Finally, they passed the phone to Mother.

She stood up and reached for the receiver, stretching the black cord over the desk.

"Alo," she said in Romanian. After exchanging a few sentences, Mother then passed the phone back to the man seated behind the desk, who continued the conversation.

She sat down, silent, eyes fixated on the white wall in front of her. From the look on her face, I could see something was wrong. But I dared not ask. It would be weeks before mother would tell me the terror she faced as a result of that conversation that day.

Chapter 17

Several minutes later, two more men entered the room. The one behind the desk seemed to be in charge. After telling the others something, he then stood up, walked around to where we were seated and motioned us to follow him.

Once outside, he walked around a white van with the side doors wide open.

Inside the van was a long bench covered by a white sheet. A small light bulb dangled from the ceiling, hung loosely by a black thin wire, reminiscent of an Alfred Hitchcock movie. Sterile and cold, it gave me an eerie feeling.

The tall man motioned for us to enter. Stepping up and over the threshold, we bent our heads, entered the van, and took our seats. Next to us sat our only belongings—the shiny orange duffle bag with nearly nothing inside.

Enclosed behind those doors, I felt darkness envelop me. Until that moment, I had not realized there were no windows. No view to the outside. No means to look beyond those doors.

Up until that point, no matter how difficult our journey had been, there were always windows. There was always an opening that pointed to somewhere. There was always a horizon—something I could yearn for, look for, focus upon. But now?

I felt as though the only thing staring me in the face was darkness. Looking at the closed door in front of me, I felt my eyes water and wondered what was going through my mother's head. Neither one had said a word for what seemed like an eternity.

"Mama, I'm scared," I finally uttered, breaking the silence. "There are no windows here."

"Don't be scared," she said, holding me tightly. "Look, over there!" she said, pointing to the back of the van. "See that grill? It's small, but if you concentrate, you'll be able to see a little bit of heaven peeking through it. If you focus on the light, Sperantza, you won't feel the darkness around you. Just focus on the light."

Sure enough, on the back wall to the left was a small grill about 7 centimeters long and perhaps 4 centimeters wide. Locking my eyes onto the small ray of light that shone through, I felt as though I could breathe again.

Outside, I could still hear the men's voices and footsteps. With each one, the sounds seemed to fade farther and farther away. Then, there was silence. Within minutes I heard quick, short steps nearing the van, a screech as if a door had opened and then a thump. I felt the van shake a bit. Finally, I heard the sound of the engine starting as we drove away to who knows where.

We rode and rode for what felt like a long time. I wasn't sure if the distance was long, or if it just seemed that way. I felt as if we had been on the road forever.

Mother remained silent. She was no doubt praying for our safety. I tried to focus on the small ray of sunlight—my only connection to the outside world. Somehow, I felt more at ease until that fateful moment when I heard a resounding noise.

The van came to a stop. I heard men's voices again. I, then, heard what sounded like gigantic, heavy, iron gates being thrown open. The sound reverberated in my ears. Boom! Boom! Boom! It was as though huge iron hammers pounded upon steel. Overwhelmed by emotion, I exploded into tears.

"Mama, they're going to kill us!" I cried out loud. Burying my face in her bosom, just like a baby chick would under her mother's wings, I couldn't stop sobbing.

"Shh! Don't be scared," I heard her say, her voice cracking. "Let's pray, just pray...." Holding me tightly, she began: "Father, please...." Silence.

Wondering why Mother stopped in mid-sentence, I slowly pulled away to look at her. Through the dim light that hung above our heads I could now see her face. She looked so pale.... Mother had always been so strong. If she had any fears during this entire ordeal, I never knew it. But now, her eyes were shut. Her lips quivered.

Pulling me back towards her chest, as if not wanting me to see her in such a state, she gently kissed my head. And with each kiss, I felt another wave of Mother's love.

She finally whispered, "Please help us, Father, please. Protect us..."

And then, I heard that sound again. Boom! Boom! Boom! That heavy-iron-gate-sound hitting against cement walls echoed in my ears once more.

Head buried in my mother's chest, I awaited my death sentence.

Chapter 18

The van came to a stop and I heard the engine shut off. My grip tightened around mother's waist. She squeezed me even closer as she wrapped her arms around me. I could hear my heart thumping against my chest, ready to jump out. My temples throbbed and I felt as though my head was ready to explode.

A barrage of tormenting thoughts ran through my mind. "Did the woman at the restaurant not understand what we wanted? Did I make a mistake? Did I choose the wrong words?"

Suddenly, the door pulled open. We were inside a room. The van was actually parked inside a room with carpet on the floor. We froze. I don't know what our faces looked like. Without a doubt, fear and desperation must have been written all over them.

"Bună Ziua. Nu vă fie frică. Sinteţi in siguranţă! Sinteţi pe pămint American, Doamnă." Good afternoon. Don't be afraid! Don't be afraid! You're safe now! You're on American soil, Madam.

Hearing Romanian words spoken by this tall, distinguished gentleman with curly salt-and-pepper hair standing before us, with a beautiful smile on his face, was like seeing an angel from God. We couldn't believe our ears. Did he say we were safe on American soil? We were incredulous.

Seeing our reluctance to exit the van, he kindly extended his arms to help us out. Continuing in Romanian, he said: "Come out. You're safe now. Trust me! You are on American soil."

Stepping outside the van, my eyes were drawn as if by magnets to the pole in the corner of the room. I kept walking, but my eyes remained fixated upon what stood erect as a sentinel at attention. Draped in a cloth of red, white and blue, there she was—the American flag—the symbol of the country that had always represented freedom and liberty for all—The United States of America.

I wanted to scream for joy. I wanted to shout because of happiness. The roller-coaster of emotions I had experienced for the entire day, however, left me with just enough strength to barely whisper, "Thank you, God."

Chapter 19

My name is Mr. Johnson. Please, sit down. Relax. You are at the Information Headquarters and have been brought here for your safety. I assure you that no one will harm you here."

"Thank you, sir," Mother said, holding back her tears.

He walked behind a desk, sat down, and continued, "This is simply a process you must go through. It will last approximately three to four days. Once completed, we will take the next step. My photographer will come and take a picture of you, so you can at least have an I.D. Then, I will need to ask you some questions."

With a click and a flash, the photographer took our pictures and was gone.

"Are you ready?" he asked.

"Yes," Mother answered. Seated next to her, I swallowed hard. "What was he going to ask me?" I thought. "What if I don't know how to answer his questions? What will happen then? What if I give the wrong answer? What then?" And as if he had read my mind, he looked at Mother and said, pointing to an overstuffed beige leather seat:

"Your daughter may sit on the couch. How old is she?"

"Fourteen. She's only fourteen, sir."

"She's a minor, so I won't need to ask her any questions," he continued.

"So, you relax," he said, looking at me, smiling.

"Thank you sir," I sheepishly responded.

Then the barrage of questions began:

"What is your name and your daughter's name? Have you ever been a member of the Communist party?"

"No sir, I have not."

"What about your husband?"

"No, sir. He has not either."

"What about your parents?"

"No, my father was very much against the Communist regime. He was a noble man who fought for the rights of the people ever since I can remember. Working as a director for the Romanian Railroad Company at Curtici, he risked his own life and jeopardized the freedom of his own family by helping hundreds of Jews to escape the Holocaust. During his shift, my father would receive the Hungarian refugees who had sought shelter in Romania to escape the Pogroms, which had begun against them. He would hide them in his railroad cars. Then he would accompany them to Arad where, within several days, they would receive fictitious Romanian documents. My father would then place them back in the trains and accompany them all the way to the welcoming centers in the capital—Bucharest—where they would depart to various countries.

Before leaving for Israel, the President of the Jewish Orthodox Community in Arad acknowledged my father's heroic efforts through a letter he sent to him in 1948, thanking him for the humane efforts demonstrated in the salvation of Hungarian Jewish refugees from Hitler's infernos."

"Your father is a brave man. I assume your brother and your sister have not embraced the Communist beliefs either?"

"No, sir, they have not. As a matter of fact, the reason why my brother risked his own life in swimming across the Danube to escape Romania just a few weeks ago was because he had been approached by the Securitate to become an informant. Instead, he chose to flee. My sister and brother-in-law requested Political Asylum in Austria not too long ago. So, all our family has been scattered trying to escape this awful regime."

"I know these are difficult questions, but please understand we are at the height of the Cold War. We must be cautious."

"I understand, sir."

"What did you do in Romania?"

"We owned our own business. We were photographers."

"So, you didn't lack economic means?"

"No sir. That is not the reason why we escaped."

"Then, tell me why? Why are you seeking Political Asylum?"

"Sir, we are Seventh-day Adventist Christians and we want to freely worship God. Our family suffered much under the communist regime. As adults, we were somewhat equipped to handle the pain and the humiliation. But when the attacks extended to our children, we had to take action."

"What do you mean?"

"Our daughter, Sperantza, suffered a great deal of persecution as a result of choosing God. Her entire future depended upon whether or not she would attend school on Saturdays. Because she chose God, she received the daily wrath of teachers whose Marxist ideology was that of the majority."

"I'm beginning to understand a little bit better now. Where did you live?"

"In the City of Braşov."

"Ah, Braşov! I've been there. What a beautiful place, at the foot of the Carpathian Mountains. It's more like a ski resort. Now, beside your husband and your parents as immediate family, who else do you have in Romania?"

"My youngest daughter, sir. She's only four. I'm sorry, I'm so sorry," Mother said, her voice breaking, trying to contain her composure.

"It's all right. It's perfectly all right. Take your time, please, take your time. Does your husband know you won't be coming back?"

"Sir, we planned this together," Mother finally continued. "I would have never left without his approval. He has no idea if we were successful, though. The motor coach won't be back in Romania until tomorrow."

"So, you haven't contacted him yet."

"No, sir, we have not."

"I think we'll stop for today. We'll continue tomorrow. That way, you and your daughter can get some rest. Our driver," he said, pointing to a man of medium height, dressed in a white linen shirt, "will take you to the Balkan Palace Hotel."

Pulling out 200 Turkish Liras, he continued, "Here is some money for dinner. The hotel has a restaurant there as well. Please buy some food for you and your daughter."

"Thank you, sir," Mother said softly.

"Now, I want you to take a good look at our chauffeur because he will be the one who will also pick you up at nine o'clock tomorrow morning. Please, be very careful. If anyone else approaches you and tells you otherwise, do not listen. Do not speak to anyone. Do not follow them anywhere. Remain on the hotel premises at all times and wait for our driver. He will be there. You have my word. This is for your safety, you understand?"

"Yes, sir."

"Till tomorrow then."

As we stepped back into the same van, I was no longer scared. Through his kindness and gentleness, this man had managed to ease my fears. I couldn't wait to get to the hotel. Visions of luxury had already formed in my mind as I pictured my room at Balkan Palace. What I encountered, however, was something I never expected...

Chapter 20

Entering the hotel, we made our way through the semi-lit lobby. Music blared in the background while lots of men, most in what looked like naval uniforms, talked and laughed out loud. We were the only females there. As we entered, their penetrating gazes felt like fiery darts hitting my body. I didn't dare look up.

After the driver picked up the key for our room, we followed him up the raggedy wooden stairs winding to the second floor. Our heels made an echoing sound as they hit the hollow staircase. I quickly realized this was no luxury hotel. As a matter of fact, the only grandeur in this place was in its name—Balkan Palace.

Standing in front of a tattered, scratched, beaten-down, brown-wooden door, the driver handed us our key. As Mother opened the door, I gasped. My eyes scanned the room. No carpet. No nightstands. No bathroom. Nothing, except two rickety-looking beds covered in dirt-colored blankets, which looked like something I had only seen in movies—those ugly, coarse, mud-looking bedspreads soldiers used to cover themselves with while sleeping in their barracks during wartime.

"Don't worry," said Mother, as if reading my mind. "We won't be here long."

I felt like throwing up. I didn't even want to touch that bed, much less lay on it. But, I had no choice. I was so exhausted. Taking off my shoes, I finally climbed up and laid on top of the covers. I didn't dare pull them back for fear of what I might find underneath.

"I guess this is the best there is for us now. This is what we deserve," I muttered softly. "We have no papers. No money. No country... no home. We're just nobodies in somebody else's land."

"You listen to me now," said Mother, climbing in bed next to me. "We will always be somebody, and not simply somebody, but somebody special. No matter what happens, no matter the circumstance, no matter where we end up, we have value and worth. Do you hear me? This room, this place, as ugly as it may be, does not make you who you are, Sperantza. Do you understand?"

I nodded quietly.

"Who you are lies deep inside of you. It's hidden in the profoundest crevice of your soul, and no circumstance or any human being can ever take that away from you. You are a precious child—not only in my eyes, but in God's eyes. Remember, He sent His Son to die for you. And the nails He bore while on that cross are a forever reminder of the immeasurable love He has for you. Carved in the palms of God's hands—that is how much you are worth!

He has taken care of us so far. Do you think He will forget us now? He won't. He can't, my child, because He promised not to. God always keeps His word! He is 'the Truth, the Way, and the Life' and He said, 'I will never leave you nor forsake you.' No matter how dire our circumstance, we must trust. We must believe, and we must hope that He will make a way, just as He said. Don't you forget that, Sperantza. Don't you ever forget that!

I know this place is a far cry from what you have been accustomed to. This is only temporary. A day or two here, maybe three; then we'll move on. Come on, chin up," she said, lifting my head upwards. "Look out there. God has given us a window. We can look through it, beyond our circumstances. For that, we must be grateful. Just look at that breathtaking sunset. It looks like a ball of fire dipping into the black velvet Marmara Sea. Look at those ships. They're leaving the harbor, you know. They're sailing on to new and exciting places. And you must do the same. Through eyes of faith, you can envision the awesome things God has in store for you."

With those words, she climbed off the bed and walked towards the orange duffle bag. Raising it off the floor she said, "Mommy has some dried fruits she bought at the Bazaar. Do you want some?"

"Yes, please," I whispered.

"Look," she said, pulling out some Chocolate Halvah. "This is fresh."

Mother kept taking out more and more goodies: chocolate covered hazelnuts, filberts, cookies, salted peanuts. I had forgotten that she had bought all those little snacks.

As I ate, I stared out the window. Mother was right. "I do have a choice," I told myself, "I mustn't focus on this place. I must look beyond here and now to what will be and what is to come."

Chapter 21

The following day, I awoke to the sound of ships' horns as they sailed in and out of the harbor.

"What time is it, Mama?"

"It's almost eight o'clock. We must get going..."

"Is there a bathroom around?"

"Out in the hallway. It's filthy. I'll come with you."

Crossing the hallway, the putrid stench of human waste shoved me back. But, my full bladder left me no other choice but to enter.

"I warned you, it's bad," said Mother.

"This is not bad, it's awful!"

"Quick. In and out. Here," she said, pushing open a door.

Trying to hold my breath, I stepped into the stall. To my amazement, there was no toilet. Just a hole in the floor with two foot rests on each side, where I could plant my feet and position myself.

"That's a Turkish toilet," I heard Mother say.

"Yuck," I said, dashing out of there, gasping for fresh air.

"You didn't wash your hands."

"Oh, I can't Mother. Not in there."

"I have some water in the room. I'll pour some out for you, so you can at least rinse."

A few minutes before 9:00, we made our way down the stairs into the lobby. Except for the clerk tending the counter, it was rather empty. The only sounds to be heard came from a television. We looked around, waiting patiently for our driver.

Not long after, we saw the white van parked outside. Our driver got out and motioned us to follow him. When we arrived at the Intelligence Center, Mr. Johnson greeted us in Romanian again.

"Bună Ziua, I trust you've had a good night's rest?"

"Yes, we have. Thank you," responded Mother. I had another opinion, but Mother had taught me well enough to know that this was not the place nor the time to elaborate on the hotel's quality, or lack thereof.

"Sir," she continued, "here is the money you gave me yesterday. It's all there. We didn't use any of it," she stated and handed him back the Turkish Liras.

"What do you mean? What happened? You did not eat?"

"We had a few snacks in our room," Mother replied timidly.

"Mrs. Totpal, I gave you that money so you and your daughter could eat a hot meal. Don't tell me you didn't eat breakfast either?"

"Ahhh, no, sir. We did not."

"You must be starving!" he exclaimed.

With those words, he reached for the crystal bell seated on his desk and rang it. A young man entered the room. Mr. Johnson told him something in Turkish and then he turned towards Mother.

"Mrs. Totpal, that money was for your food. You didn't need to bring it back."

"I know, sir, but we didn't use it. It was simply the right thing for me to do."

"I understand and I appreciate your honesty. But I want you to keep it.

Very well, now. Let's continue the process we began yesterday. I have some more questions for you."

I quietly listened as the debonair gentleman asked Mother question after question. As I watched him write down her answers, I could see that he was moved by her plight. Half-an-hour later, the young man returned to the room, this time carrying two trays of food in his hands.

"Ah, finally," Mr. Johnson said, "Here is some warm food for you. I have a few things I must do outside the office. Please stay here, and eat in peace. We'll continue afterward."

"Thank you, sir," Mother and I responded, almost in unison.

"Mama, look!" I said, uncovering plate after plate: "stuffed red peppers, piping-hot vegetable soup, warm crusty bread with butter just the way I like it, luscious black olives with feta cheese, cookies with chocolate on top, and, ahh...my favorite...baklava. Oh, and there is peach nectar, too. This is a feast!"

"Isn't this wonderful?" I asked, glancing up at Mother. Wiping away her tears, she simply nodded, "Eat my child, you just eat."

For a moment, I hesitated. I wondered why she was so pensive. What was she thinking?

Father still hadn't heard from us. By now, the motor coach would have arrived back in Romania. And he, no doubt, would have been informed that we were missing. But he still didn't know whether we had been able to escape—if we were dead or if we were alive.

Was Mother thinking of my adorable four-year-old sister, who would be without her mommy for who knows how long?

The hunger pangs I felt in my stomach, however, mixed with the delicious smell of food snapped me back to reality, forcing me to refocus. To my stomach's delight, I began to eat.

"This gentleman was indeed a God-send," I thought. His benevolence was touching. Although his job was one of great importance—in essence to verify whether we were spies entering the country or honest refugees trying to escape a diabolical regime—his treatment towards us was beyond reproach.

"Did you have enough to eat?" he asked upon returning.

"It was more than enough, sir. Thank you so much."

"Mrs. Totpal, here are some papers I need you to sign. As I had mentioned earlier, the interview process usually lasts between two to three days. I have verified all the necessary information regarding your family and feel I can make my decision now. I believe what you have told me is the truth. I will keep you here no longer. Instead, I will begin processing the papers necessary for you to be admitted into the Refugee Camp."

"Thank you very much, sir."

"The camp is located in the Asian side of Istanbul. You are now in Istanbul's European side. The same driver who brought you here this morning will drive you to the port. He and his van will then accompany you on the ferry, taking you across the Bosporus. Once on the other side, he will drive you to the Refugee Camp."

"How long will we be there, sir?"

"It's hard for me to say. I don't know exactly how long. But you will be there for at least three months, possibly longer. I want you to understand, this is a process and it requires time. Political Asylum is not granted easily. There are immigration laws, investigations, rules and regulations that must be followed in order for you to receive such status."

"What about my family, sir? What about them? When can they join us?"

"Mrs. Totpal, the only status you have right now is that of a refugee. Unfortunately, those rights are extremely limited. Once you are granted Political Asylum, we can request legal immigrant status and entry into the United States. Then, and only then, will you be in the position to request the reunification of your family."

"That could take months, couldn't it?"

"I don't want to discourage you, but, at the same time, I don't want to lie to you either. The Romanian government is a tough one. A typical family reunification can take up to five years."

"Five years? That's not possible," Mother said, bursting into tears. "What about my little girl, sir? Can't you do something? Anything? She's only four."

"Madam, I will do everything in my power to help you. I promise. I will call the Red Cross and explain your plight. Maybe, just maybe, they can help expedite this process. But, you must remember, this is not an easy path. Freedom does not come cheaply, Mrs. Totpal, as you have, no doubt, already experienced. There is a high price for those who wish to attain it. But you mustn't give up. You have journeyed too far to give up now. Keep focused. Don't forget you are the only pillar of strength your eldest daughter can lean on during this ordeal. Stay strong for her."

Gathering her composure as she got up from the chair, Mother stepped toward the door. "Thank you, sir," she whispered as she looked back. "Thank you."

"Did I hear him right?" I thought to myself. "Did he say five years? Five years? No, it couldn't be possible, simply not possible...."

Chapter 22

As we entered the van once again, I felt an incredible mix of emotions. Excited to see my new home, yet anxious about how long I'd be there; happy for reaching yet another milestone in this freedom process, but scared about the prospect of being separated from my loved ones for so long.

"Mama, do you really think it will take that long to see them again?" I asked.

Mother's gaze seemed far away. I'm not sure if she even heard me. I didn't dare ask her again for fear of making her cry. So, I remained quiet for the rest of the journey.

At the port, we followed our driver onto the ferry, climbed the stairs to the third level, and slid along the shiny wooden benches to our seats by the window.

"Mama, look!" I exclaimed excitedly, pointing to a large plateau below us. "Those people are driving cars onto the boat." I had never seen such a thing. Mini vans, mini-buses, and cars of all colors and sizes were being neatly parked one behind the other onto an immense parking space. "Do you think the van is there, too?" I inquired.

"It's possible," answered Mother. I noticed that her voice was very quiet.

"That would be so cool, if it was," I blabbered on.

Young boys who didn't appear older than 10 or 12 years old carried baskets full of huge, ring-shaped sesame pretzels on their shoulders, as they entered into our compartment. Their voices were quickly drowned out by those who followed behind them selling drinks and all sorts of other trinkets: accordion post-cards, t-shirts, bags, gum and candies. Each one tried to out-do the other, vying for that one more customer.

As I looked around me, I was impressed by the striking contrast of the people: business men dressed in impeccable suits and elegant attachés, engulfed in reading their newspapers seated next to others whose clothes and mannerism cried loudly of such meager means. Young, beautiful women dressed in gorgeous, ultra-modern clothes mingled with those whose bodies and faces were covered up from head to toe.

Suddenly, the waves began convulsing, and the boat rocked vigorously from side-to-side.

"I feel so sick, Mama," I groaned.

"Do you want to go the bathroom?"

"No, I just want to get off this boat," I responded.

"Me, too, Sperantza, me, too. Please be patient just a little bit longer. Look, I can see land. We're almost to the other side."

Holding my breath as much as I could, I mumbled to myself, "I won't throw up. I won't throw up. I won't throw up."

Grateful to be off that boat, I watched in amazement as the driver jumped into the van, as it rolled off of a large, automated boat plateau.

"Wow, Mama, this is incredible!" I said. The largest boat I had ever seen prior to that point was the size of a canoe. This was certainly the beginning of many new things.

Getting back in the van once again, we rode for several kilometers. When we finally arrived at our destination and the driver opened the doors, we stood in front of a two-story building behind wrought iron gates and a heavily-armed guard. Opening the gate with a large key, the guard—a tall, mustached Turk—smiled at us. As he nodded his head, with his hand on his chest, he said, "Gemal. Gemal." We assumed that "Gemal" was his name. We nodded and followed him into the building and up the stairs to what was to be our new home.

Gemal opened the smoked glass door that led into a large room. Lined up against the wall were six single iron beds. On top of each, was a dirty-looking, bluish-gray-striped mattress, reminiscent of convicts' uniforms. Forcing a smile on my face, I turned my head, only to be shocked again by the life-size graffiti plastered on the opposite wall. As hard as I tried, my eyes couldn't filter out the obscenities and drawings of indecently exposed women that filled the otherwise empty space. Although I had not yet developed a keen sense of art appreciation, I quickly realized this was definitely not art. This was degrading, disgusting, and distasteful.

Mother and I just stood there. Neither of us could utter a single word. For a moment, my mind transported me back to my own room at home. I saw the wooden floor covered with Persian rugs, my beautiful walnut furniture, the treasured bookcase that held my favorite authors, my desk in front of the large window overlooking the back yard, my own radio and, oh, my comfortable bed dressed in white damask with overstuffed goose-down pillows.

"Ein moment," I finally heard Gemal say, snapping me back to reality. I had forgotten he was still there. He left the room and returned minutes later with a tall, thin gentleman.

"Bună Ziua, Doamna Totpal. Mă chiamă Medet." Hello, Mrs. Totpal. My name is Medet.

"Bună Ziua."

"You may wonder how I know your name. We spoke on the telephone a few days ago when you were at the Police Grand Station. I don't know if you remember. Gemal wanted me to tell you this is the only room available in the camp. Perhaps in a few months, as other refugees vacate the premises, there will be a private room available for you. Until then, you will have to share this space with four others who will be arriving soon."

"I understand."

"Oh, and another thing. He also wanted you to know he is sorry about the graffiti on the wall. He wasn't expecting a mother and young daughter to arrive in a place like this."

Gemal handed Mother a room key and sort of bowed his head as if in respect. He and Medet, then left the room.

I remember standing there, almost transfixed. Looking out through the large window, I gazed into the horizon and remembered Mother's previous words. "This place, this room, does not make you who you are, Sperantza. You have worth. You have value. You must look beyond your circumstance, beyond the present, to what will be."

And then it dawned on me. A window! Once again, it was that opening to another realm, to another space in time, which helped me see things from a new perspective. It had happened all along—in my grandparents' villa, on the bus, in the hotels, in the van—windows to possibilities seen only with eyes of faith encouraged me.

It was as if God had gone ahead of us in this journey and carved out these openings for our very own eyes to help us see beyond our present circumstance and give us hope. Hope in spite of present danger. At that moment, I felt assured that no matter how difficult this journey would continue to be, His presence would always be streaming through a window.

Chapter 23

Mother and I took the beds closest to the door. A small, wooden night stand stood between the two. Above the beds near the window, was a clothes line, which stretched across the room. There was no armoire or closet space I could remember. But then, again, why would we even need one? The only clothes we owned were those worn on our backs.

Facing each other, we sat on those beds, for how long, I do not even know. Mother had her head buried in her hands, and I held mine, as if I were her mirror image.

"Did someone knock?" I finally asked, lifting my head. Mother shook hers.

There was silence. Then the knock came again. Jumping off the bed, I reached for the door handle and opened it.

"Bună Ziua, I am Mrs. Diaconu. My husband and I live in the room next door, and we couldn't help but overhear when you came in. We're glad you're..."

That was all she managed to say, this motherly-looking woman, before the flood of tears held inside of us for so long gave way, interrupting her sentence. As Mrs. Diaconu took one step closer and opened up her arms, Mother and I felt drawn to her as if by an invisible magnet. Burying our heads in her chest, we just sobbed.

"Shh. Shh. You will be fine. You will see. You will be fine. Shh. Don't cry now. Don't cry," she'd say over and over again, just like a mother trying to comfort her crying baby.

The warmth of her embrace reminded me of home. It felt like an eternity since we had left. And then, as if I could endure yet still more pain, it dawned on me that "home" as I had known it until then, was no longer home for me; because a true home was the one place where, no matter how long I had been gone, I could always return. And finding myself in this room, this place, this refugee camp, was certainly not home....

"This is just temporary," I heard her say, finishing her sentence, as though she could have read my thoughts.

"Temporary, temporary." The word echoed in my ears, its meaning becoming clearer. "She's right," I thought. "No, this is not home, but it will have to do until that day when I will reach the place I can call home again." And with that thought, I wiped the tears off my face and stopped crying.

"Thank you," Mother said. "Thank you for coming. My name is Michaela, and this is my daughter Sperantza. I'm sorry," she said, wiping off her tears, "The past several days have been quite difficult."

"How old are you, child?" Mrs. Diaconu asked me.

"Fourteen."

"Fourteen? My Lord, how in the world did you manage to escape Romania with a fourteen-year-old? Come on, I want to hear your story, but it's almost dinner time. My husband and I will show you around the compound."

Mother locked the door behind us. I wondered why, but then remembered we had one thing of value there—our camera. Stepping outside the building, we walked down and then up a few stairs to a covered sidewalk that led into a rather large, dark room set up with tables and chairs. To the left, near the small windows, were two ping-pong tables. Four white balls rested against the net on top of two orange paddles. To the rear, above what looked like an opening in the wall, hung a television playing a Turkish program.

"This is our entertainment room, our cafeteria room, our everything room. It's multi-purpose. Ha, ha, ha," Mr. Diaconu chuckled. "This is the place where we spend most of our time." A kind-looking, soft-spoken gentleman, Mr. Diaconu was in his late 50s.

"As you can see, we have a lot of time on our hands. There is not much else we can do while we wait for our papers to be processed. We've been here for two months now, but we're told we'll be leaving soon. Madame Vivienne said so."

"Who's Madame Vivienne?" asked Mother.

"Oh, that's right, you don't know her. She's the refugee camp director. You'll meet her, very soon, no doubt. She's the one who ultimately decides how long you'll stay here and when you can leave."

"What do you mean?" Mother inquired.

"He means, she has the power to keep you here for as long as she wants to," chimed in a man, disgustedly, who was standing behind us. "I've been here for months. This is a business. She makes money off of us. That's why she keeps us here, to make money off of us. I'll never leave this place at the rate I'm going..."

He kept rambling while the line of people waiting for food kept moving forward. As we reached the niche in the wall, Mother and I picked up our tray of food and found a place to sit next to Mr. and Mrs. Diaconu.

"His name is Simon," explained Mr. Diaconu softly. "The poor man has been here for eight months. He's gotten really sick and no country will take him in until he gets better. It's a sad situation. Every time someone else arrives or leaves, not only is he reminded he's still here; but, worst of all, that he's been here the longest."

After dinner, Mr. and Mrs. D., as we began to call them, introduced us to several couples. We met the architects from Bucharest, Romania, a husband and wife in their late 20s who were waiting entry into Canada; George and Florin, best friends and marine officers in their 30s, also from Romania, who spoke fluent English, headed for Canada as well. Then there were the Bulgarians—one lanky and olive-skinned; the other, short, red-haired, freckled and cross-eyed. There was Traian, the cook who had jumped off his ship to escape, and the Schmeltzers, a Romanian couple of German descent, with no children who were awaiting entry into West Germany.

"Who's that?" I whispered, pointing discreetly to the strange-looking man outside?

"Oh, that's Ilich," said Mr. D. "He arrived a few days ago. We were told he escaped from the USSR. The guards say he apparently ran on foot across the border and was shot at by Russian soldiers. He's scary-looking, I know."

"He looks more like a mad man," I said.

"There's a reason for that. We heard that after crossing the border, he lived in the woods for weeks, wounded. When the Turkish border patrol finally found him, they thought he was dead. How he survived it is beyond me. It's a miracle. He can't talk to anyone because he's the only Russian here. He just nods as he walks by and stares a lot. He's very much alone."

"Why is he covering his mouth?

"He has no teeth. I think he's embarrassed, so he does that all the time."

"Mama, he really scares me," I whispered.

"Just don't go near him, Sperantza. He won't do anything to you."

After dinner, Mr. and Mrs. D. showed us around the courtyard. We walked back to the covered sidewalk, which connected to the main building, and then around to the front near the gated entrance. As we turned the corner, we almost bumped into Gemal who was seated on a bench reading his newspaper. Greeting him, we kept on walking.

"Ein moment," he called out to us. "Medet! Medet!" he yelled.

Medet came running. "I need you to stop by my office, before you go back to your room. I have some things to give you," he translated.

"Danke schön, " I responded, without even realizing that my little bit of German came in handy.

"Bitte," came the response.

To the right of the building, underneath a large tree and seated on a few chairs, we noticed several men playing chess. Not far behind them, against the fence that encircled the entire camp grew some wild vegetation.

"This is it," sighed Mr. D. "As I said, there's not much to do in this place."

"The good thing," added Mrs. D. "is that, if we're good, we're allowed to leave the compound for a few hours during the day, with prior permission, of course."

"If we're good?" asked Mother puzzled.

"Yeah, they assess our behavior," said Mr. D. "How we act with Gemal and the rest of administration and how we get along with the other refugees. They watch us, you know. Based on that, they decide whether or not to grant us a pass. As a matter of fact, just last week, several men broke out in a fight while playing a chess game. Within a couple of hours, Gemal had several police officers on site, and, within full view, they began beating them with their batons. It got really ugly. They've also been sequestered for an entire month. Frankly, I feel that even their departure has been jeopardized."

"I don't think it was just that, though," said Mrs. D. "These men have been constantly complaining, at least since we've been here, about everything— from the food, to the living conditions, to Madame... And, as they say, 'the walls have ears.' "

"Whew! That was a lot to handle," I thought. I felt my head spinning once again. So, if the "walls had ears," that meant I still had to be careful with everything I said and did. Although we were on our way, we were still far from being free.

"Please forgive us. We are exhausted," said Mother. "We'll be heading back to our room, if you don't mind. Have a good evening."

"Good idea," said Mrs. D. "You need a good night's rest. We'll talk more tomorrow. We're not going anywhere anytime soon," she said, laughingly. On our way up, we stopped by Gemal's office. On top of his desk were pillows, covers, and sheets.

"Für sie," he said, as he placed them in our hands.

"Danke schöen," I responded.

Holding them close, as I climbed up the stairs to our room, I couldn't remember having ever been so grateful just for clean sheets.

Chapter 24

The following morning after breakfast, Mother approached Medet whom she later found out was a Romanian Turk from the island of Adacale, a Turkish colony on the Danube Delta in Romania.

"I need to make an urgent telephone call to my husband. He must be frantic by now, not knowing what's happened to us. I don't even know where to begin. I wonder if you'd be kind enough to help me since you speak the language."

"Mrs. Totpal, the only place I know where you could make an international phone call is from the main Post Office. It's on the European side. We must request permission to leave the compound. Let me find out if there is a group leaving for Istanbul this morning. It's much safer if we travel in larger groups since you have no formal identification. There have been some shootings and unrest in the area, so we must be careful."

With a nod, Mother continued up the stairs. I followed. Entering the room, she opened the orange duffle bag and pulled out the only valuable thing it held. Opening the camera carefully, I saw her gingerly removing the money Father had hidden for us in the film spool—300 Deutsch Marks. "This must last us for as long as we are here," she said, almost introspectively. "I don't know how, but it must." Placing the money in her purse, she said, "Let's go, darling. We are calling Daddy today."

Downstairs, outside of Gemal's office, people were waiting in line. Medet was just coming out.

"Here's your signed permission slip for you and your daughter, Mrs. Totpal. I explained your situation to Gemal, so I'll be taking you to the Post Office. The Schmeltzer family and several others are going also. We'll stick together."

"Thank you, sir."

Leaving the refugee compound that morning was exciting. I couldn't wait to hear my daddy's voice and tell him we'd made it, that we were alive, and that we were on our way to freedom!

Walking on that dirt road up the hill, we passed by what looked like a school building. The bell rang, and, within seconds dozens of little ones dressed in blue and white uniforms rushed out for recess. Their energy and laughter was contagious.

Suddenly, I caught a glimpse of Mother's gaze. Holding onto the bars of the wrought iron fence that encircled the building stood an adorable little girl. She couldn't have been more than six. With eyes like marbles set in a most beautiful round face, chocolate brown hair down to her shoulders and pulled back by a sparkling white bow, she looked more like a china doll than a real child. She stood there for a little while, head tilted to the side, watching us. She then smiled, waved, and ran off to play.

"What a cutie," I said. "She looks just like..." but then, catching myself, I stopped in mid-sentence.

Mother half-smiled and then sighed sadly, "I know," she said. "I know. That's exactly what I was thinking, too," she said, sighing again.

"This must be heart-wrenching," I thought. My little sister, Cornelia, is almost that little girl's age.

I couldn't dwell on the thought too long since we had reached the bus station and Medet was already making his way into the mini-bus.

"There is no space," I said out loud.

"Get in, get in," he said. "This is Turkey. They'll make space if they see you coming. They'll squeeze. Right there, sit down," he said, pointing to a tiny space open on a seat. "Mrs. Totpal, there is a space right behind her. I'll stand," he said, holding onto the rail handle.

Good thing he did, because that driver took off like a mad horse in a race. I just prayed, hoping I'd get out of there alive.

"Don't be scared," said Medet, seeing my face. "They're good drivers. You'll get used to it after a while."

When we finally got off the mini-bus, I couldn't believe how many other people stepped out.

"We'll be taking the tramway, then the ferryboat, then the tram again," Medet said. "It's quite a ways away. That's why I insisted that we grab that first Dolmus, as they call it. We must be back on time."

"Mr. Medet, here are all the Turkish Liras I have," said Mother, handing him the money she'd received a couple days before while at the Intelligence Headquarters. "For the tickets. I will need to exchange some money before getting to the Post Office."

"Why don't we do something else instead," he suggested. "I will lend you the money to make the phone call, and then we'll go to a friend of mine, Ali, who owns a store in an Istanbul district not too far away. He'll give you the best exchange rate."

After more than two hours of traveling, we reached the Post Office. Medet spoke to the receptionist and then turned to Mother. "What city are we calling, Mrs. Totpal?"

"Breaza, the city of Breaza, in the Prahova County, Romania."

"And the telephone number?"

"It is 101. The Negreanu Family."

"Dad must be at Buni's house," I thought. Beside my aunt and uncle's apartment, this was the only other place that had a telephone.

115

We sat down and waited. Each time the receptionist made an announcement, I'd jump up, startled, thinking it was for us. Then I'd stare back at those shiny, wooden telephone booths lined against the wall. Watching the people come in and out through those glass doors, I wondered when we would be next.

After almost an hour, Medet said, "That's you, Mrs. Totpal. They've got the connection. Romania, booth number 7."

Mother jumped to her feet and dashed to the phone booth. I followed. Pulling the door open, she entered and picked up the receiver. "Alo, Alo, Cornel, da, dragă eu sint." Hello, my dear, it's me, it's me.... That's all she could say before her tears choked her, making it nearly impossible for her to speak. Holding the door open, I had every intention to step in. But, hearing Mother break down and weep, I let it close instead.

"Oh, God, give her strength," I whispered, standing there, looking on.

It felt like forever until she managed to utter her next words: "We're... we're fine," she'd say, between sobs. "Yes... I'll write. I'll tell you everything. I love you! Kiss my little one for me. Tell her that Mommy loves her and will see her soon."

"Soon," I thought, "would not be nearly soon enough!"

Seeing her hang up that receiver was like watching a movie in slow motion. She looked as though she wanted to capture that moment, to freeze it in time and never let it go. She just stood there, longingly looking on.

"Let's go, Mama," I finally said, opening the door.

She tried to smile but, deep down inside, I knew her heart was crying. Wrapping her arms around me, burying her head in my hair, I heard her whisper, "Daddy loves you so much."

Chapter 25

M r. Ali, a tall, bearded, kind-looking gentleman who sold furs and clothes supplied merchandise for various countries throughout Europe.

"This is Mrs. Totpal and her daughter, Sperantza," said Medet. "They have just arrived in the Refugee Camp yesterday."

"Nice to meet you, madam," he said in perfect Romanian.

"What a relief! You speak Romanian." Mother said. "I would like to exchange some Deutsch Marks. Mr. Medet said you'd give us a good rate."

"Of course. How much do you need?"

"Just 50."

As Mother spoke to him, I was drawn to the rows of clothes, beautifully displayed in his store. Oh, the extravagant furs were a sight to behold. And then the jeans. There were piles and piles of them. In Romania, I had never seen them in a store. Every now and then, I would see someone wearing them, but, with a price tag of 1,000 Lei, or one-third of a professional's monthly salary, jeans were a rarity. Besides, the only way you could purchase them was through a foreign source. And here I was, standing so close,

I could almost touch them. But I didn't dare. All I could do was look, in hopes that maybe I would someday also own a pair.

"Mr. Ali, how much for a pair of jeans?" I heard Mother ask.

Did I hear correctly?

"She could surely use a pair since all we have are the clothes on our back, since our escape."

"Let me get a few sizes down for you," he said, kindly.

"Try these on Sperantza," Mother said, as she handed me several pairs.

"Mama, what do you think?" I asked, coming out of the fitting room.

"Those fit perfectly. We'll take them, Mr. Ali," Mother said, pointing to the dark blue pair."

"How much are they," she asked?

"Let me see," he said, grabbing them from Mother's hand. Looking them over he exclaimed, "Hmm, there is no price tag on these! If there's no price tag, there must be no price."

"Mr. Ali, please," said Mother with a small smile on her face. "Tell me how much I owe you."

"You don't owe me anything, madam. Medet told me briefly about your situation. While you were in the dressing room, I called my wife, and we decided to do this for you. Frankly, neither she nor I can imagine what you must be going through—a woman refugee in a foreign country, separated from your family. What's a pair of jeans compared to that? Oh, and by the way, when you need to call your family, you can do it from here. Free."

Mother and I stood there speechless. Here was a man whom we had just met, and his wife, whom we had never met, both wanting to help us.

"Sir, I don't know what to say..." said Mother, her voice trailing.

"Please say yes. When our family was in need, others helped us too. This is our way of giving back."

"Thank you, sir. Thank you."

Leaving Mr. Ali's store that afternoon, I felt he was no longer just Medet's friend. His kindness and compassion rendered him ours as well.

"You missed supper," Gemal exclaimed in a stern voice, opening the iron gate.

"We're very sorry sir," Mother responded.

Looking at his watch, he continued. "But you made the curfew. That's important."

With barely a few minutes to spare, I thought, but we did.

"And your family? Did you contact them? Do they know you are well?" he asked.

"Yes, sir, we did. Thank you for giving us permission to go. May God bless you. Good night."

Thanking Mr. Medet once again, Mother and I went up to our room where sleep overcame us in no time.

Chapter 26

Over the next several days, we became acquainted with more and more people. Hearing their stories, it was evident they had escaped the communist regime in search of a better social and economic life. Then the inevitable question would arise. "What about you? Why did you escape? And how?"

Mother would then share her faith and the incredible risks our family took so that we could worship God. It was during one of those conversations that we met George and Florin. These two Marine Officers, who had jumped ship during the night while their vessel was crossing the Bosporus Strait, were intrigued.

"I don't understand," said George. "Why would you want to risk your life, your family, your future, everything for God? How do you know He even exists?"

"Someone once said," responded Mother, " 'No one is willing to die for something they believe it is not true.' But let me ask you George, why did you risk it all?"

"With me it's different. I'm single. I have no family. I have no ties. I simply wanted to lead my life the way I wanted, with no one watching over my shoulder and no one telling me what to do. I was exasperated by the communist regime, and I saw the possibilities abroad. I wanted that lifestyle. I wanted those things."

"You see, George, you were willing to sacrifice your life for things. We were willing to sacrifice our lives also, but for a different cause."

"That's what I don't understand. He's invisible, yet He has so much power over you, to detach you from your family and disturb your way of life? For what? A belief in someone you haven't even seen, and are not sure even exists?"

"George, my God is real. I can't convince you of that fact. That's something only He can do. What I can tell you, though, is that He loves you!"

"Loves me? Yeah, right," George said, sarcastically. "You don't know what I've done. You don't know the kind of life I've lived. You've been a Christian all your life. If He loves you, that's one thing, but me? He has no reason to love me."

"We've all done things we are ashamed of. The Bible says that none of us are good. We have all sinned and have fallen short of the glory of God. That's why we all need a Savior. That's why Jesus came two thousand years ago—to save us, to forgive us, and restore us back to Him. He left everything He had to rescue all who had been lost, by paying the utmost, highest price—His own life. When He died on a gnarled wooden cross that Friday so long ago, He did it for you, too. He bought you with His blood, George. That must be worth something."

Florin, the other officer who had been quietly listening, hung his head low. "She's telling you the truth, George," he finally said. "God is real. I know I've never mentioned this to you, but I grew up in a Christian family as well. Believing in God under our Communist regime was too much of an inconvenience for me. The pressures were much too strong. I wanted position and status in my life, just like you. I wanted economic security. And I could get them all, I thought, if I'd only forget about Him. But those things couldn't fill me. There was still emptiness in my soul.

What I'm realizing now, listening to this woman talk, is that He's never forgotten me. In the darkest times of my life, He was still there, patiently waiting for this very moment—the courtyard of a refugee camp, no less—for my eyes to be opened to His infinite love. That's amazing. I know I've been ashamed of Him. I know I've let Him down. Yet, in spite of all I've done, He's still willing to forgive me.

How do I know that, you ask? Because I once remember reading a text somewhere in His Word saying that if my sins were red as crimson, He will make them white as snow. I don't understand it, and I can't wrap my mind around it, but I must believe it because in that same Bible, He also said He is the Truth. So, if He's willing to do that for me, George, how much more will He do for you? You didn't even know He exists."

Silence followed. Mother and I stood there waiting for his response. Head tilted to the side, George sighed deeply and said what none of us expected.

"Can you teach me more about Him? I want to know about Him."

Chapter 27

Life in the Refugee Camp was monotonous. Every day, we began with the same breakfast: a cup of tea, two slices of bread, feta cheese, and a few black olives. The food was hand delivered, literally. Several men carried colossal trays on their heads or on their shoulders for several blocks to the Refugee Camp. For lunch, most of the time, we had stuffed peppers or Turkish Musakka, (a dish prepared with sautéed eggplants, green peppers, tomatoes, onions, and minced meat) served on rice-pilaf.

After several days eating the same thing over and over again, I felt so sick of the food, I didn't even want to see it again. With the little money we'd receive from the monthly allowance, Mother would go to the nearby market and buy tomatoes, cucumbers and onions to at least prepare a small salad we could eat.

After breakfast, we were free for several hours until lunch. Thereafter, we were free until dinner—free to wonder about the camp, to read, to write, play ping-pong, or to watch television. Most chose to do the latter.

After several weeks in the camp, I felt as though time was passing in slow motion. I thought, "If this is what it will be like for the rest of our stay here, it will be very difficult."

One afternoon, Mother and I entered the dining room where cartoons were playing on T.V. It looked like "Tom and Jerry." Florin and George began to laugh.

"What does it say," asked someone? It says, "Follow me!" they responded. It was obviously funny and, at that moment, it dawned on me that George and Florin understood English. How I wished I could understand it, too.

As if they had read my thoughts, the following morning the two Marine Officers announced, "We have decided to teach a beginners English class. We are far from fluent, but we'll teach you what we know. It can give you a head start and since there's not much we can do in this camp anyway, we might as well make ourselves useful. So, whoever is interested, we will start tomorrow morning at 9:00."

In a Refugee Camp of close to 100 people, only a handful spoke English. There were the Marine officers, the Yoga-practicing Bulgarians, and the architects.

The following morning, Mother and I were seated in the first row with our pen and paper ready and eager to learn. Seated behind and beside us were several others who were just as interested as we were by this offer. What a blessing those hours became to us. Every day, we looked forward to that time where our minds would be stretched and, in the process, opened to this new, beautiful, yet complex language. Little by little, we began learning the pronunciation of simple words, conjugating verbs, tenses, and constructing and writing sentences.

Time began passing quicker. New words, new understandings, and new discoveries unfolded before our very eyes. It wasn't just a new language, but really a new world.

For the next several months, George and Florin continued teaching us what they knew. In the end, it was a wonderful exchange. They taught us the beginnings of a new language, and Mother unveiled to them the greatest language ever told—a love language written in red on a cross long ago when "...God so loved the world that He gave His only begotten Son, that whosoever believes in Him should not perish but have everlasting life."

Chapter 28

If we could only find a church in this city." mentioned Mother one day. "What a blessing that would be." It had been weeks since we had gone to church. How I missed the fellowship and love I once felt there.

"Do you think there could be one?" I asked in unbelief.

"I don't know. We are in Turkey, after all. Mosques are the prominent places of worship here, and remember what we've seen on the streets!"

"I'm still in awe at how these people just bow down to the ground no matter where they are, even on the streets, at the call to worship. Not once, or twice, but several times a day, too."

"They are very devout and reverent," Mother said. "Maybe Medet can help us."

"Mrs. Totpal, I must admit, I haven't heard of many Protestant churches in Istanbul," he responded. "But, although Muslim, Turkey is rather modern and quite secular. Who knows? I'll speak with Gemal. Maybe he can help."

A few days later, Medet handed Mother a piece of paper. On it was the address of what he thought was the church. We were thrilled!

"I must warn you, Mrs. Totpal, trying to find this place will not be easy. More than likely, it will be hidden from view, in an obscure location for security's sake. Please be careful! You shouldn't go alone. There's a lot of unrest on the streets. As a matter of fact, yesterday, one of the refugees was caught in the midst of a group of armed university students as he was heading back to camp. He barely escaped."

"I appreciate your concern. We will be careful."

With Gemal's permission in hand, early that following Saturday, Mother, George, Florin and I, all headed out in search of the church. It was a crisp September morning. The sun was shining, but the wind was cutting through the thin layer of clothes I was wearing. We took the Dolmus—the mini-van taxi transportation—to the dock where we boarded the boat that crossed over the Bosporus to the European side of Istanbul. Once there, we walked and walked for miles trying to find the place, but to no avail.

"Do you think this place exists?" I finally asked Mother.

"I don't know, Sperantza, but if it does, I've prayed that God would help us find it. We'll keep looking."

It was evident the place, if, indeed, we could find it, was not easily accessible. George and Florin were on a mission, though, and nothing seemed to deter them from their goal. Turning from one street to another and then yet another, crossing through sometimes 14 lanes of oncoming traffic without so much as a pedestrian crossing or demarcation lane, they wouldn't give up. "Taksim. We need to get to Taksim," they would say. In English, in German, in Italian, whatever language they could use to make themselves understood, they used.

After several hours of walking and searching, we once again zig-zagged our way through a myriad of cars, vans, trucks, and taxis beeping their horns, desperately trying to reach the other side without being hit. In front of us stood a hill with many buildings. Hundreds of steps wrapped around it, making a way up to the top.

Slowly and methodically, we climbed, and climbed, and climbed some more.

"Mama, I can't take one more step, I'm so tired. My feet hurt."

"Just a few more steps, Sperantza, we're almost there," Mother would encourage me.

As we reached the top, we followed the sounds that led us to the sanctuary through the heavy, carved wooden doors. The building was rather large, but only a handful of people were inside. We slipped reverently onto the last pew, hoping not to disturb the service. But, within seconds, all eyes were on us. A few minutes later, a short, stocky, kind-looking gentleman wearing an obvious toupee came toward us. "Do you speak English?" he asked, in a British accent.

"Yes, we do," responded George.

"Welcome! We have an English Sabbath School, and I would be delighted if you joined us."

We followed him to a separate room. Florin translated for Mother and I. Then, we returned to the sanctuary for a three-way translation. The gentleman translated from Turkish into English, and George continued the message into Romanian.

I don't remember what the sermon was about. All I knew was how blessed I felt to be there. Just hearing the familiar sounds of hymns and being surrounded by other Christians was indescribable. At the end of the service, the pastor and his wife came and introduced themselves.

"My name is Ohanis Delice, and this is my wife. We're so happy you've joined us. You must honor us with your presence and stay for lunch."

Their apartment was a few meters away, further up on the hill on the right hand side. It was nothing luxurious, but impeccably clean. Sitting in their kitchen around the large square table, facing the three wide windows that overlooked the neighboring flats, felt so much like home again. The aroma of the food being warmed up permeated throughout the intimate area, making my head spin.

I know there were several courses Mrs. Delice served, but what I will never forget were those fresh-from-the-oven puff pastry turnovers filled with delicious cheese that melted in my mouth. Had I had no shame, I would have polished off the entire plate, but Mother had taught me better. Her nudging elbow discreetly reminded me to restrain myself. So, I politely took one more, eagerly wishing one day I would eat them again.

"Where are you from, and how in the world did you find us?" asked the pastor.

Thus began a long, animated conversation that lasted throughout the meal and into the late afternoon. For the next few hours, I felt like I belonged again, like this was my extended family I had never met. Growing up, Mother had told me about the "Body of Christ," as she called it—the family of believers spread throughout the world, but I had never understood what she really meant until that day.

"We're so glad you came," said Mrs. Delice. "I know I speak for my husband as well when I say that as long as you are here in Turkey, our home and our church are yours, as well." And indeed, they were.

Sabbaths had always been special to me, but they became even more so. They were like an oasis in the middle of a desert land. They were the highlights of my week and I couldn't wait for them to arrive. Through that experience, I realized how God's love transcends language, culture, race, and nationality. God's love unites us no matter where we find ourselves in the world. Isolated, but never detached. Lonely, yet never alone. Saddened, but never forgotten.

Chapter 29

I t was late November already and we had been in the Refugee Camp since June. The weather turned colder in September. There was no heat in our rooms and no insulation whatsoever. None of the doors and windows closed properly. The cracks between them were so large, we could hear and feel the wind blowing and whistling through them.

Mother had endured those conditions for all the months we had been there, but now the pain and swelling in her face had become unbearable. No teas, warm compresses, or over-the-counter medicine worked.

"We must take you to the dentist," said, Mrs. D. Have you seen your face? You must have an infection."

"I can't go, Mrs. D. I have no money for a dentist."

"Well, the camp will have to do something. This is an emergency. I'll tell Gemal. Michaela, you should have complained a long time ago." With that, she indignantly obliged.

Mother was grateful for all she'd been given. Gemal had been so kind to us. She would have never complained. Thanks to Mrs. D, however, that very day, Mother was taken to a dentist who did all he could to alleviate her pain. Unfortunately, the long term damage was already done. As a result of that awful infection, Mother would lose several of her teeth within a few short years.

"You must keep warm, Michaela," said Mrs. D. that evening. "And you must rest. I brought you a heater. An electrician here in camp made one for us. I asked him to make you one, too. Be careful, though. Don't get electrocuted!"

"Electrocuted?" I thought. Getting a closer look at the rudimentary contraption built from two red bricks and a piece of wire, I quickly understood the warning.

"Remember, keep it out of sight. When Gemal comes to check your room, hide it. Should he find out we're consuming energy, we'll all be in trouble for it. He's been known to revoke bath and laundry privileges for much less."

"Anything but that," I thought. The once-a-week, barely 30-minute time slot was already such a rare privilege, that the mere possibility of having our bath and laundry time revoked was enough to make me want to cry. The rules were strict. A posted warning on the weekly sign-up sheet read: "Be punctual! Those who aren't must wait till next week!"

Even at the risk of losing such "luxury," I knew Mother needed to keep warm in order to get well.

"I'll keep an eye on that heater," I heard myself say to Mrs. D as she was leaving.

"You do that honey. Oh, Michaela, I almost forgot," she said, turning around. "You know the Schmeltzers."

"How can I forget them," whispered Mother, "especially after what happened to Sperantza and I downtown."

"When?"

"Last week, when we had permission to go to town. I must have forgotten to tell you. The Schmeltzers were with us. As we walked, we noticed two young men coming from behind. We thought nothing of it, but then it became very obvious they were indeed following us. We changed directions several times, and so did they. When we finally came to a stopping point, they approached Sperantza and asked if she spoke German."

"I told them I didn't.

"Do you speak English," they pressured.

"No."

Then, looking at me intently, one of them exclaimed: "Ich liebe dich!"

"Mrs. D, I was so shocked I didn't know what to say. Why would someone I had never seen in my life tell me he loved me? All I could respond was, 'Why?' He began to tell me something I couldn't understand, so the Schmeltzers stepped in to translate. He told them he loved me, and wanted to marry me. I was so scared. Mrs. D, it was just crazy. Mother told them we were going to America. But he was persistent. He told the Schmeltzers he had finished the university, had a career, could pay Mother the money for the dowry, and that he really wanted to marry me.

'I could take you to my parents' home right away so you can meet them,' he said.

If it weren't for the Schmeltzers who communicated with them in German, like Mother said, I don't know what we would have done. Even after they explained at length that I was only 14, wasn't ready to get married, and that we were going to America to continue my education, they still followed us for quite a while."

"By that time, I was concerned about a possible kidnapping," Mother continued. "We decided the safest thing to do was to make our way back. I began praying silently for God's protection. As we turned the corner, we ran into another large group from Camp and told them what happened. Almost immediately, we found ourselves surrounded by this human chain that kept us safe as we continued walking. When we finally got to the dock, those two were gone. So, I will be forever grateful to the group, and especially to the Schmeltzers."

"That must have been frightening," said Mrs. D. "I'm so glad the Schmeltzers were with you. You know, earlier today they received word their Visas were approved. They'll be leaving for Germany shortly. I wanted to tell you that when they do, my husband and I will take their room, and you and Sperantza can take ours. It's much warmer and the walls are much cleaner."

"Oh, yes!" I thought. How can I forget those walls in our room, filled with filth we tried to ignore for months, but whose impact chipped away at my innocence each time I saw them. Not to mention the embarrassment I felt, every time someone walked into our room and saw those walls for the very first time.

"Wouldn't that be wonderful, Mama, to move out of this place? I can't wait," I said, climbing into bed next to her, hugging her tightly.

"Yes, it will, darling. It certainly will."

Closing my eyes, I prayed silently for God to make Mama well soon.

Chapter 30

You have a package waiting in my office," said Gemal to Mother the next day. "It arrived earlier this morning, but I haven't seen you till now. I'm heading back there in a few minutes, if you want to stop by."

"A package?" said Mother. "From whom?" she wondered out loud.

A large, white, square-shaped box sat there, wrapped with thick brown tape with the word "Austria" written all over it, covering nearly half his desk.

"It's from Auntie Lia! It's from Auntie!" I exclaimed. "She sent us a care package."

Excitedly, we carried it up the stairs and into the room, tearing it open with such anticipation. Inside were shirts, skirts, underclothes, shampoos and deodorants. "Mama! Look, hazelnut chocolates," I said, pulling several bars out of the box. "And cookies! Lemon wafers and chewing gum. This is heavenly! Oh, Mama, this is incredible! I can't believe it. Look at these clothes!"

I picked them up, one-by-one and I held them close against my body. I was almost afraid to let them go for fear of losing that privilege again. For weeks on end, I had been wearing either my little summer dress I had on the day of our escape or the pair of jeans Mr. Ali gave Mother. If it weren't for Mrs. D who sowed Mother the green skirt she always wore and a warmer top, she would have been worse off than I was.

"We'll have new clothes to wear now, Mama, new clothes!" Although I could tell these were not new, they were new to me, so it didn't matter. I was grateful to have them and for my Auntie Lia who had sent them to us. In my excitement, I didn't even notice tears trickling down Mother's cheeks until she called my name.

"Why are you crying, Mama," I asked, coming closer. "Aren't you happy?"

"I'm overwhelmed, my sweetheart. Come here, sit down," she said, pushing away some of the clothes to make space for me next to her, on the bed. Then, she began reading me a most beautiful letter that I can only summarize, but whose impact will last forever in my heart.

My dearest little sister,

Words cannot express the joy of hearing how God helped you escape safely out of Romania. I can't wait to hear the rest! Nicu and I are in a Refugee Camp in Traiskirchen, Austria. They treat us well here. We have even found work at a ski factory in Tyrol.

Last week, a group of Pentecostal brothers and sisters came to visit and brought us lots of clothes. I put together whatever I thought you could use. The only thing missing were shoes.

Taped at the bottom of the box, underneath the clothes, you will find some money in a small envelope. I send it to you with all my love. Be strong! Be courageous! Know that God is always near and that we will meet again soon!

Until that day, remember, I love you with all my heart.

Your sister, Lia

P.S. I almost forgot. Emil wrote to me. He found a sponsor, and his papers have been approved. He will be departing for America within a couple of weeks. We hope to join him soon. Love you much!"

"So, Uncle Emil will be the first to set foot on American soil!" I exclaimed. "Then Auntie Lia and Uncle Nicu, then us. I can't wait! I just can't wait! Dad and sister will then join us, and this ordeal will all be behind us."

"Well, this is what I wanted to speak to you about, Sperantza, but I don't know where to even begin. I heard some awful news this morning. We might have to go back."

Chapter 31

W hat do you mean, 'we might have to go back?' To Romania?"

"Listen to me, Sperantza. Ceaușescu has apparently issued a decree to stop all reunification of Romanian families abroad. If that is the case, he leaves us no choice. We must go back. I cannot live without Dad and Cornelia. We cannot live apart."

"Mama, do you understand what you're saying? Do you understand what they'll do to you if you go back? I'm at least a minor. But you? What will happen to you? They will beat you. Torture you. At the very least, they'll put you in prison. I don't even want to think about the worst.... I wish I could kill that Ceaușescu, Mama. Strangle him with my own hands. Boil him alive so he'll get a taste of the pain he's inflicted on all of us. He's not human. He's a devil from hell.

Mama, listen to me," I continued, kneeling down in front of her, holding her trembling hands, "I..., I can't go back! I just can't! I... I won't! If you want to go back, then you go, but I can not. You must have someone outside of that place to help you get out, one day."

Until that moment, I had never dared speak a word contrary to my parents' wishes. I had been raised with an incredible sense of respect and obedience toward them, and to say what I had just said was shocking, even to me. I didn't know where those words came from, but I believed them with all my heart. I was convinced there was no turning back. My only choice was forward.

Poor Mother had to process not only the devastating consequence of a possible return, but also what I had just said. Incredulous, transfixed, she tried hard to fight back the tears.

"Mama," I said, shaking her a bit. "God will make a way. He's on our side! He'll never leave us! Remember, you've always told me that? He didn't bring us this far to abandon us or tear us apart. Somehow, He will make a way."

As I got up off the floor, I leaned over her. Touching her face ever so gently I tried to wipe her tears, but the tremor in my hands reminded me of how scared I really was.

Surrounded by the things that had brought indescribable joy and happiness, just moments before, I, now, stood there astonished, facing the possibility of being separated not only from my father and my little sister, but also from my beloved mother.

Chapter 32

The uncertainty of the days that followed were grueling—a constant reminder of how fragile our new found freedom really was. Mother didn't know what to do. Calling Father to discuss such matters over the telephone would have been unwise. Besides, all international phone calls were tapped and he was under constant surveillance because of our defection.

If, indeed, this rumor was true, how could she possibly prepare him for what would happen upon her return? But, if it wasn't and she questioned him about it, the communists would have accomplished their objective in the intricate mind game they played. Their goal was to instill fear in people, and get confirmation that their diabolical idea had actually worked.

Our safest option was to rely on outside sources—someone who lived in a free country who could confirm whether or not the rumor was true. But who?

Mother had already shared her concerns with several people, but none could ease her worry. Their response was typical, "One never knows what to expect with Ceaușescu. It could be a scheme, but who could really know what to think of this deranged man whose only goal in life is the maddening pursuit of his own cult of personality!"

Every day, we continued praying, asking God to bring someone into our lives who could answer the question.

"The package!" Mother exclaimed one day. "The package Auntie sent us, where is it? We need her address. Did you throw it away?"

"No Mama, it's under the bed. I use it for my clothes, since I have nowhere else to keep them."

"I just remembered Auntie has some friends in Vienna who can verify this information through Radio Free Europe."

How could I have forgotten that short-wave program? For those of us living behind that wretched Iron Curtain, it had been our only link to the free world.

"That would mean more uncertainty for at least a few more days, till we hear back from her, wouldn't it, Mama?"

"Yes, I know, but at least then we would have an answer."

For the next week, I dared not broach the subject again. In my childish mind, I somehow thought that if I didn't speak of it, the pain would just go away. But it didn't. Night and day, the thought of being separated from my mother haunted me. In my mind, I had reasoned there was no turning back. But, in my heart, the thought of being alone absolutely terrified me. I felt so scared.

Until the day we left Romania, I had never been apart from my family. Surrounded by my grandparents, aunts, uncles, and cousins, ours was a family that cherished and celebrated every single moment of joy together. For the past several months, however, living in this Refugee Camp had marked my life with deep and painful scars. I didn't know how I could possibly bear more. At times, I wondered what Mother felt but didn't dare ask.

Day after day passed, and then weeks, until one morning, when looking out through the cafeteria window, I saw Gemal running frantically toward the building. As he entered, he said, "Michaela, quick! You have an international phone call in my office."

Mother sprang up! I jumped to my feet and ran behind her like a fawn crossing a field.

"Alo," said Mother as she grabbed the receiver, trying to catch her breath.

"Lia," she said, bursting into tears. She couldn't say much after that. But I could hear Auntie's voice on the other end through the receiver. "Michaela, don't go back! It's not true. What you heard is not true. Promise me you won't go back! Promise me. They will kill you if you go back. Those are just Ceaușescu's tactics of intimidation."

"I won't. I promise," Mother finally managed to utter between sobs. But before she could even say goodbye, we heard the loud sound of the dial tone abruptly bring the conversation to an end.

Resting her head in her hands, Mother did not move. I stood there beside her, hearing my own heart pounding, as if it was ready to jump out of my chest. Not even Gemal dared interrupt this moment. Respectfully looking on, he remained outside his own office. He had heard the rumors of the mad man, Ceaușescu, and probably sensed this was the moment of truth.

Mother rose to her feet. Her voice filled with emotion, she finally said: "They're not true! The rumors are not true! Praise God, they're not true!"

"That was my sister, from Austria," she continued telling Gemal. "Ceaușescu has not passed the decree to stop the reunification of the families. He has apparently tried, but was unsuccessful since such a law would be a direct violation of the human rights agreement he had previously signed."

"Oh, Mama, I'm so happy you won't leave me. I'm so happy," I said. Throwing my arms around, I felt like a little orphan child who had just found her long-lost friend.

That night, for the first time in weeks, sweet sleep deeply enveloped me, only to wake up the following morning to the challenges I had yet to face.

Chapter 33

S perantza, you must stay inside today," said Mother. "It's very cold and you can't go out wearing those things." The burgundy, open-toed sandals Mother bought me in the Bazaar on the day of our escape were the only shoes I had left. Mother was right. I could feel the cold draft blowing through the window cracks. This was not sandal-wearing weather.

A few days before, when visiting Madame Vivienne's office for more paperwork, Mother had told her I needed shoes. "It's getting cold and damp. I'm afraid she will get sick, wearing those sandals."

"Of course," Madame Vivienne responded in a kind voice. "My assistant will come and pick you up next week."

A very elegant, chic, French lady in her early 50s, who looked more like a movie star than an administrator, Madame Vivienne was the director of the Refugee Camp. She single-handedly held the power to decide our fate—how long we would remain in the Refugee Camp, how fast our paperwork would be processed and how quickly we would be transferred to our next destination.

So, after being stuck inside for several days, the morning when Madame's assistant was to arrive came with much anticipation. I couldn't wait for the moment he would take us to the stores. I had passed by those windows where merchandise was elegantly displayed. Every time we would visit Madame's office, and every week we went to church, my eyes would delight in the beauty of the shop windows. There were leather shoes with intricate designs, and purses that matched to perfection. There were suede ankle boots that came in endless colors, crocodile leather belts with shiny golden buckles, and clutches of every shape. They almost took my breath away.

I knew those stores were expensive. I saw the prices, which were elegantly displayed, through the windows. But, further down the street, the merchandise was much more affordable. Each time we passed one of the stores, I hoped we would enter.

"Maybe this is the one," I wished silently. Passing store after store, however, my hope grew dim.

After walking for several kilometers, Mr. Nadir, Madame Vivienne's assistant, stopped in front of a narrow door. He pulled it open, and we entered into what looked and smelled like a shoe repair shop. On the shelves, piled up on top of each other, were used shoes with yellow tags sticking out.

I saw no pretty colors like in the other stores we had passed. There were no matching purses displayed upon cascading fabrics in huge windows. There were just plain, drab, ugly shades of brown—dark and monotonous brown.

After the usual niceties with the shopkeeper, Mr. Nadir motioned me to sit down. The owner measured my foot and then disappeared behind the black curtain. Deep down in my heart, I still held on to a little bit of hope that he'd return with a pretty pair of shoes. But when I saw what he gave me to try on, I felt like crying. I had always liked brown, but this must have been the ugliest shade of brown I had ever seen. The shoe style was similar to a loafer-type that my own grandmother would not have worn, much less a teenager.

As I stepped out of that place I was unsure of what to do: wear those hideous things and keep warm, or my pretty, worn-out sandals and get sick. I believe it was at that time that my desire for beautiful shoes began as I made up my mind that this would be the last time I would ever wear an ugly pair. Mother, on the other hand, politely thanked him, and then we said goodbye.

"See you next month," he replied.

"I hope I'll never see you again," I mumbled under my breath.

Chapter 34

Within days, however, my wish was quickly shattered when the black Rolls Royce he rode in pulled up the hill and stopped in front of the gate. When the chauffeur got out of the car and opened the back door, we knew it was her. "Madame is here. Madame Vivienne is here," people whispered throughout the Camp. Walking right behind her was Mr. Nadir, her trusted assistant.

"Why is she back so soon?" I thought. A refugee group just left the camp last week.

"This can't be good," another person remarked.

"She never comes this often," said someone else.

We all gathered around, with bated breath, waiting anxiously for her announcement. Any time Madame arrived in Camp, it was always an event. Most often she came to announce the list of those fortunate ones who had found a sponsor and had been approved for their departure. Other times, she carried unfortunate news for those who had been denied entry or had no one to sponsor them.

For the past six months, we had witnessed the process so many times that we had learned her routine. Madame would pull out her black leather cover dossier and begin reading the names out loud. Next, she would pause a bit. She would then smile, and say, "Visa approved." And then, she would announce the country accepting that particular refugee.

The names she read last on the list were almost always the ones denied. Each time it happened, there was a sense of mixed emotion in the air. I didn't know whether to rejoice with those who had been approved or cry with those who had to wait another month in this forsaken place.

Simon, the man who I thought sounded quite deranged the first day we arrived in Camp six months ago, stood in front of us. Placing his right hand over his mouth, he tried hard to suppress the awful cough he had developed from pneumonia. Each month, it seemed as though his name would be the last one to be read, and each month, the verdict was the same: "Entry denied."

"I wonder if I'll ever get out of this place," he mumbled, with a sad smile on his face as he passed us by. Seeing him so thin and frail-looking, with his back hunched and head down, moved me to tears. "Poor man," I thought. "He could be my grandfather.

"Will anyone ever accept him?" I whispered to Mother.

"Only if he gets better, honey. No country will ever take him in as long as he is sick."

"But how can he get better if he has lost hope?"

"Shh," said someone behind us. "She's not done yet."

"Of course she is," I thought. "If she read Mr. Simon Dima's name, she must be."

"Maybe next month," whispered Mother, wistfully, as she got ready to leave.

"Maybe..." I said, trying to sound matter-of-fact, until I heard Madame read our own names.

Until that day, I had never heard our names read out loud. At only 14, and the only child there, I wasn't prepared for such blatant rejection. The emotional impact of not only being denied, but having it announced in front of all those people was more than I could bear.

I burst into tears and dashed upstairs. Throwing myself on the bed, I cried uncontrollably. Curled up in the fetal position, I didn't even hear Mother walk in until I felt her hand gently caress my back.

As I turned toward her I could tell she was trying to explain what happened, but I couldn't stop sobbing. She wrapped her arms around me, holding me tightly. When I finally quieted down, she cupped my face in her hands. Looking me in the eyes, she said, "Darling, we have been approved! We've been approved! We're leaving for Italy in a few days."

"We've what? Approved? You really mean it, Mama? We're really leaving this place?"

"Yes, we're leaving on Thursday."

"That's in only two days!"

One might have thought I'd just heard worse news because I began bawling all over again. But this time, there were tears of joy.

Chapter 35

I don't remember anything else after that moment, until Thursday arrived. Even that day was a blur. What I will never forget, however, was the anticipation that I felt arriving at the Istanbul airport as I walked to the Alitalia gate and waited to board our plane to Rome. I had never been on an airplane before, so I was excited!

Several of us, refugees, were traveling to Italy that evening. A gentleman from our group, seated nearby in the boarding area asked, "Have you ever seen a dollar bill?"

"No," I responded, sheepishly.

"Here, take it," he said, handing it to me. "They say it's good luck to hold it in your pocket when you arrive in a new country." As he shook his head in disbelief, he added, "I'm still amazed at how you two have survived the Refugee Camp. It's tough enough on men, let alone a woman and a child. Let's hope Rome will be a better experience for us all."

"Thank you," I said, holding this new treasure in my hand.

"Ladies and gentlemen, your attention please. Our flight to Rome will be boarding momentarily."

"That's us, Mama! That's us!" I said excitedly, jumping to my feet. As we made our way into the airplane, we found our seats near the middle. Seated by the window, I couldn't wait for takeoff. The flight attendant, a tall, distinguished, middle-age gentleman arrived and helped us with our seatbelts. I sunk back comfortably into my seat. I still could not believe it. Was I really leaving, never to return to that Refugee Camp again? Was this really happening or was it a dream? Feeling the thrust of the airplane push me back on takeoff, switched my mind forward. "What next?" I wondered.

"Oh, God," I whispered, "whatever happens next, please, don't let it be worse."

Drifting to sleep, I later awoke when the captain announced our final approach into Rome.

"Look outside," whispered Mother.

In the deep, dark night, millions and millions of lights seemed to cover the ground. They looked like flickering candles. Mesmerized, I pressed my nose against the window and relished the fairytale-like scenery until we touched the ground.

Chapter 36

We got off the plane and made our way to the exit through customs and immigration, where we were shocked to see Traian and the Bulgarians, who had left the Camp a couple of weeks before us. They were standing in the waiting area.

"Welcome to Italia, Mrs. Totpal," they said, smiling. "Welcome!"

"How did they know we were coming, Mama," I asked?

"I don't know! But it's so nice to see familiar faces."

A striking young woman with flawless olive skin and long, curly ebony hair, stood next to them, carrying a dossier. She motioned our group to move in closer and began speaking in English, but with a very heavy Italian accent.

"Buona Serra! My name is Francesca Benini, and I am from the World Catholic Church Services. Welcome to Italia! For tonight, we will place you in a Pensione, so you do not worry. Tomorrow morning, however, you will have to report to our headquarters in Roma where you will receive the necessary instructions and paperwork for your stay in Italia."

"Mrs. Totpal," she said, "I understand your friends here have already made arrangements for you, so you will be going with them. The rest of your group will be coming with me."

"Don't worry, Mrs. Totpal," said the Bulgarians, "we already have a place for you. It's a three-bedroom apartment we rented in Lido di Ostia, not too far from Rome. Traian is in one room with us. A Czechoslovakian couple with an eight-year old girl is renting the other. The third bedroom was vacated a couple of days ago, so we thought we should reserve it for you."

"I thank you so much for your gesture, but, I have no money," said Mother. "How much is the rent?"

"We have spoken to the landlord, and you don't have to pay anything tonight. Tomorrow, we will take you to the World Catholic Church Services [WCC] to receive your monthly allowance. Then, you'll be able to make the necessary arrangements."

"Let's go. Hurry! That's our bus to Rome," said Traian as he pointed to the one with the motor idling. "Quick! Get on. If we miss it, we'll have to wait till midnight for the next one."

The bus was packed, but squeezing past the crowd toward the back, we found a couple seats. No sooner had we sat down when the driver sped off. He made me feel as though we were in a race car, not a bus. Each time he'd make a turn, it felt as if we were literally leaning on one side, ready to topple over at any moment. When we reached the highway, I thought, the driver had mistaken it for a racetrack because he accelerated so hard.

"Does he think he's driving a Ferrari?" I asked.

"No, he just loves speed, as most Italians do," said Traian smiling. "But, don't you worry! They're great drivers!" Just as he said that, the bus driver slammed on the brakes. Even those holding onto the handrails lost their balance. The ones who were more daring ended up on other people's laps.

"This is crazy," I exclaimed, pushing off the bag of an older gentleman that had landed on my lap.

"There's only one more bus to Lido di Ostia," said George, the Bulgarian, smiling.

"What a consolation!" I thought.

"This is our stop," said Traian. "It's the end of the line."

As I stepped outside, I felt the crisp midnight air hit my face.

"We're almost there. Just a few more blocks," said George.

"It smells salty," said Mother.

"It's the Mediterranean. The apartments are just across the street from the beach. We're home."

As he reached for his key, Traian opened the door to the apartment and then showed us to our room. Remembering Istanbul, I braced myself for the worst. But when the lights came on, I saw a room that was warm and inviting. There was real wood furniture, a real bed (not just a mattress on iron rods), two large armoires where we could keep our clothes, night stands, and pretty bedcovers. And the walls were clean!

"What do you think," asked Traian?

"Thank you! Thank you," said Mother, her voice cracking with emotion. "How can I possibly thank you enough?"

Chapter 37

The following morning, we awoke to the buzzing, sounds of motorbikes, cars, and sounding horns. As we stepped outside, we beheld a most glorious sight. Across the busy street, the sun was dawning upon the Mediterranean. Between revving Vespas and speeding Fiats, I could hear seagulls.

"What do you think," asked Traian? That seemed to be his favorite question.

"It's breathtaking," said Mother. "I'm still wondering how in the world we'll be able to afford living here."

"By the end of the day, you should have some more answers. Let's go now. George and I will take you."

We walked to our bus station and hopped on to the Metro that took us to Termini, the Grand Central Station in Rome, and on to another bus to the World Catholic Church Service headquarters.

"It's not far from here," said George, "just another kilometer or two."

Although my feet hurt, I didn't complain. I was in my own little world. Walking the streets of Rome and taking in the sights felt almost surreal. In the past, I had only read of these famous places, of these landmark buildings that had stood for centuries, representing this ancient world power. It was to this empire that my own people and my country, Romania, traced their roots—descendants of the Daco-Romans.

I heard the poetic, musical tones of the Italian language. It resonated so similarly to my own, that it made me tear up. I had always heard about the power of the spoken word and the impact it had on the formation of my mother tongue. Although surrounded by Slavic countries, Romania withstood and maintained the integrity of its Latin roots, classifying it as one of the Romance languages closest to Italian. But, to experience it first-hand felt so close to home again.

"We're here. This is the building," said Traian. "The Catholic Organization is on the third floor."

We entered a large, imposing, gray stone building, which looked as if it had existed since the beginning of time. Up the winding mahogany staircase, we climbed to the third floor. Then down the corridor to the right, we stopped in front of a massive wooden door with a golden plaque that read "World Catholic Church Services Organization." We pushed open the door and stepped inside where we were greeted by an elegant elderly lady.

"Buon Giorno. My name is Laura Buonarroti. Please come in." Although her English accent was a bit heavy, we understood her clearly. "Let's see," she said, opening a large dossier. "Michaela and Sperantza. Right?"

Mother and I both nodded.

"Well, there is good news. Good news for you, today. You will not be in Italy for very long! As soon as the United States grants you the Visas, we will be able to complete your file with the necessary documentation. I don't know if anyone told you this, but you have been granted Political Asylum due to the religious persecution you have suffered. Because of that, your case will be given priority."

"Molto bene, very well now, you will have to report to our organization every week as we work on your dossier. Do not worry. Today, you will receive some money for transportation and living expenses. In Italy, the hardest and most expensive thing to find is a place to live. Food...not so bad. But apartment, oh, mama mia," she said, gesturing with her hands. "So, good luck! Let me see."

As she said that, she leaned over her desk and punched in numbers in her adding machine. She, then, tore off the tape, which hung loosely over the top.

"140,000.00 liras for you and 140,000.00 for you. Yes, that is correct," she said, checking her numbers again.

"Here it is," she said, handing Mother a wad of paper money.

"Thank you," said Mother.

"See you next week, alora. Arriverderci."

"Arrivederci. Grazie."

"I can't believe this," Mother exclaimed under her breath on her way out.

"Now, do you understand why we said you can afford the room in Lido," said Traian smiling?

"That's more than 300 hundred dollars! Three hundred dollars! How much is that room, Traian?"

"$150."

"Per month?"

"Aha."

"Mama, in Istanbul we were given $10 a month per person! How come?"

"Well, in Istanbul we were provided with food and lodging. Here, we are responsible for those things ourselves."

"Yes, but if the organization pays a monthly set sum for each refugee, that means somebody received a lot of money."

"Sperantza, don't forget that inflation was high and the political situation in Istanbul was very unstable. No doubt, they did the best they could and, for that, we must be grateful. What I want you to remember is how God protected and favored us every step of the way. Focus on the good, my darling. Always focus on the good! God has led us and continues to do so. Look at the amazing way He found us a place to live. You heard what Mrs.

Buonarroti said—apartments in Rome are very expensive and hard to find. Yet, God had already provided for us before we even arrived."

Mother always had a way of knowing how to refocus my thoughts. She seemed to live out a quote I once read, which said, "We have nothing to fear for the future unless we forget how God has led us in the past." And led, He had. Even though the Istanbul experience had been harsh, God provided people who loved us, who were kind to us, who empathized with us, and who took care of us.

"You're right, Mama," I finally said.

As she wrapped her arm around my shoulders, she smiled and turned towards Traian.

"Do you know a place I can buy Sperantza some shoes? A place I can afford?"

"There is a flea market not far from here. You can get things there for less than ten dollars, and you can bargain."

"I don't think they're open every day," said George, the Bulgarian, "but I saw a store nearby that's reasonable. Maybe you can try there."

He was right. The flea market was closed that day, but the shoe store was not. Elated, I entered and chose a beige suede pump that tied in the front with a tassel made out of the same. I wore my brand new shoes as I walked outside of the store, thrilled to finally get rid of the brown pair I so deeply detested.

Traian and George showed us around that day. We learned our way around the supermarkets, which were immense—nothing like the ones we'd seen before. They showed us where the Post Office was located, as well as the train, the metro and the bus station. They also showed us where to buy tickets, how to get there, and so many other things.

That was the day when I also tasted my first slice of pizza—pizza al metro—as they called it or pizza by the meter. It was also then, that I savored my first raspberry-hazelnut gelato.

We returned home exhausted, late that evening. As we entered, we were greeted by the Czech couple from across the hall. They spoke little English and none of us spoke Czechoslovakian, but we somehow managed to communicate in the bit of Italian we all understood.

My heart almost melted when their eight-year old, whom I had never met before, sprang toward me with open arms. Although she looked nothing like Cornelia, I found myself embracing this little girl with big blue eyes, round chubby cheeks, and golden-wheat hair. She was such a reminder of my little sister.

As we retired to our room that evening, I couldn't help but remember Mother's words earlier. God had always provided for us. Even in the most difficult circumstances, He was there. His presence, His peace, His love, and His protection never failed us.

I happily took off my new suede shoes and was reminded once more how He was interested even in the tiniest details of my life.

Chapter 38

Life in Italy was so different from what we had experienced before. Even though Mother and I shared a three-bedroom apartment with six others, we had a place of our own and were able to take a shower every day. We had a kitchen where we could cook the food we liked and we were free to come and go as we pleased. Those simple pleasures were such a privilege.

Every morning was a fresh new experience, and this day would prove to be no different. Mother had carefully separated the money for the rent, bus, and metro. We would use the remainder for food and any other miscellaneous items we might need during the month. There was one other marked envelope Mother always set aside first. It was God's tithe, which was the ten percent she had always taught me about.

"God is the owner of it all," she would say. "Everything we have comes from Him. Even the tithe He asks us to return is for our own good, since the best antidote to selfishness is giving."

Mother had made sure she exercised my "giving muscles" since I was only a child. I remember how she would teach me to always give away the biggest piece of anything I had—be it a rare chocolate, candy, or a cherished fruit. At first, that was very hard; but, with time and effort, it became a habit. What amazed me the most that morning was Mother's faithfulness. Even though we knew of no church where we could give the money to, she set that envelope aside, gently placing it inside her Bible on the bottom of her drawer.

She then turned toward me and asked, "Sperantza, do you remember if the supermarket is far from here?"

"We could walk, Mama, but it would take us a while. If we go on the bus, it's about seven stops. I counted them yesterday."

"Let's take the bus," she responded. "It's faster. Not to mention easier, especially when we come back carrying those groceries."

Walking to the opened kiosk covered in a collage of newspapers and colorful magazines, I purchased two round-trip tickets. The bus arrived shortly and, in less than ten minutes, we were there.

As we made our way through what seemed like endless rows of food trying to decipher what was what, I saw Mother suddenly stop. She pulled down a rectangular-shaped package, wrapped in sparkling golden cellophane. The container advertised the cutest little girl smiling, as she took a bite of what looked like the yummiest chocolate cake. Mother said, "Doesn't she remind you of Cornelia?"

She then placed two boxes in our cart. "I wonder," she pondered, "if we could send them a package? You know, mail them some things to Romania? I wonder how expensive that would be, or if they would even receive it."

"Let's go check, Mama," I said. "I believe the Post Office is not too far from here."

We crossed the busy street and walked past several stores in the direction where I thought the Post Office was located. Instead, we came upon a small building enclosed by an iron fence with a sign that read, Chiesa Cristiana Avventista del Settimo Giorno, Lido Di Ostia.

"Mama, look at that word," I said, pointing to the gray stone plaque. "I think this is an Adventist church!"

"How wonderful that would be!" exclaimed Mother. "Write down the address, darling, so we can return on Sabbath!"

Several hundred meters and multiple street crossings later, we came upon the Post Office building. We found out that, although extremely expensive for us, we would be able to send a package to Romania. It meant we had to restrict our food budget considerably for the month, but both Mother and I were willing to make the sacrifice for the sake of our loved ones.

It took more than six weeks for that package to reach our loved ones in Romania, but what a joy it was for them when it did. We had almost given up, thinking it never made it past the communist customs. And if it hadn't, it would have been nothing uncommon. Packages from the West disappeared on a regular basis. Since corruption was the law of the day, no one was held responsible, no explanations given. Letters were opened and read, often censored or even destroyed, never reaching their final destinations. Telephones were tapped and houses kept under surveillance, especially when flagged or marked as dissident for having contact with the West.

Daddy's situation was no different. He had confirmed to Mother in various letters through coded language only they understood, that he was not only being watched, but also being followed. He warned us to be careful, so we read and re-read every letter we sent home, checking it again and again for fear of being misinterpreted, used against him and placing him in further jeopardy.

So when Father wrote and told us they received the package, we were ecstatic. "Cornelia," he wrote, "loves the little girl on the cookie box. She saved not just that wrapper, but all the ones from the chewing gum and fruit candies as well. It's as if she doesn't want to part with anything Mommy sent her."

What made us even more joyful were the words he used in his closing sentence. "We love you and miss you and can't wait to see you!"

"'Can't wait to see you!'" exclaimed Mother, "means he's been allowed to submit the paperwork to begin the reunification process. That is amazing! Sperantza, do you remember what Mr. Johnson had told us while at the Intelligence Headquarters in Turkey? "Yes, Mama, how can I forget. He said we may not see Daddy and Cornelia for possibly five years. And now, how long before we see them, Mama?" I finally dared ask.

"I don't know exactly, sweetheart, but we'll pray and hope it won't be long."

Chapter 39

The following Saturday, we made our way back to the church building we had mistaken for the Post Office a few days earlier. This time, the gate was open. Welcomed by the joyful tunes of cheerful songs, guitars, piano, and tambourines, we entered. Nothing like the impressive sights we'd seen in Rome, this was no famous church, basilica, or century-old building. No poets had described it, nor had painters immortalized it.

But, to us, wandering pilgrims with no country of our own, this small chapel and its people would once again become the symbol of peace and safety—a place that would remain forever etched in our minds, because it made us feel like home again.

No sooner had we sat down, we were surrounded by smiling people, gesturing with their hands, speaking to us all at the same time—all in Italian.

"We're the Lautizzi family. We're the Cozzi family. We're the Gallo family."

"We are Romanian," I finally managed to respond.

"Romanian? Sorrella Vittoria DiChiara!" someone called out. "Sorrella Dichiara, veni qua!"

Coming towards us, we saw a tiny lady with wavy grayish-brown hair and kind smile. She said, "I am Romanian, also."

"Oh, what a relief," I responded.

"Where did you come from? How long will you be here?" But before we could even answer her, she continued. "You know all these families are inviting you to lunch. You must decide where to go."

"Oh, how can we?" asked Mother. "They all came at the same time, and we don't want to offend any of them."

"Well, then, I must ask them to decide who will go first," she said.

Being in that place, fellowshipping with other believers, singing, praying, and hearing God's word, even though we understood very little, seemed to transcend even the language barrier. Love is amazing that way! By the end of the service, it was decided that the Cozzi family would host us for lunch that day.

We all entered into the red Maserati—the Cozzi family and their two children, Signora Dichiara, Mother, and I.

A widow who had escaped communism and had lived in Italy for the past 25 years, Signora Dichiara could relate to our story. Trying to prepare us for what we were about to behold, she said, "You know, the Cozzi family is wonderful. They live in a villa outside of Rome. They also have a summer place near Florence, and they would like to invite you there, if your stay would allow it."

But no language could describe what our eyes beheld when Mr. Cozzi pulled into his pebble stone circular driveway. The perfectly manicured lawns, sculpted gardens and Carrara marble steps, which led to a magnificent entrance of a three-story villa made it look more like a palazzo than a house. And the immense, intricately-carved wooden door seemed larger than life. I was astounded.

Inside, I stepped onto what looked like a rectangular grand Venetian ballroom, which seemed to go on forever. Three enormous, colorful Persian rugs covered the wooden floor, which shined like glass. On the entire length of the left wall was a carved library that went all the way up to the ceiling. My eyes followed the intricate design and delighted at the incredibly detailed frescoes, which decorated the ceiling.

Settees and elegant overstuffed armchairs, covered in a rich design of paisleys, with multiple hues of burnt sienna and crisp sage green sat next to small round tables covered in a burgundy and gold taffeta, which reached all the way to the floor. On each, a fresh bouquet of flowers emanated a wonderful perfume that permeated throughout the room. A grand piano stood toward the back of the room, as if to frame the entire place. My words cannot fully describe the serenity and splendor of this home.

Growing up in Romania, I had been exposed to art and beauty from an early age, beginning with my own grandmother, a poet and painter herself. But this was no comparison. Of places like these, I had only read about in history books. But to step foot inside and be a guest of honor in this home was indescribable—moments I knew I would cherish for the rest of my life.

Chapter 40

The month of December passed quickly, between the weekly trips to the Catholic Organization, visits to our newfound friends, and sightseeing in Rome. Even the weather seemed to cooperate with our lack of winter clothes. According to the meteorological reports, it had been a very mild winter, and it would continue that way for the second week in January.

"The forecast for Rome shows a few flurries with little wind and lots of sunshine today. This is *Radio Free Europe*. Don't go away! More riveting stories when we come back."

"Free Europe?" I thought. "Mama, quick!" I called out from across the hall. "Free Europe's on." In Romania, this had been the only voice that linked us to the outside world. It was the only program that penetrated through the cold harshness of the Iron Curtain and its constant bombardment of Communist propaganda to shed a ray of hope and truth beyond its world of lies. So, here I was in Rome, months later, turning the radio dial when I came upon it once again.

"What happened?" said Mother hurrying in, hands dripping wet. Drying them off with a small terry cloth, I sat her down and said, "Listen!"

"My name is Mihai Georgescu, and I need your help. Last year, I applied for a trip to Turkey. The afternoon before the scheduled departure in June, I was told I was approved. I could already taste my freedom but, before leaving the country, while waiting for customs in Bucharest, the bus was searched and every piece of luggage removed and thoroughly checked. Except for a small hand bag that carried my essentials, I had no luggage. I became a suspect and was removed from the motor coach by the Securitate, the Romanian KGB.

After heavy interrogation, beatings, and fear-instilled tactics, I was thrown in prison where I was told I would rot for the rest of my life; all because I was as desperate for freedom as a drowning man is for air. The threats have intensified! Today, I fear not only for my life, but that of my parents. You are my only hope. Please help me!"

Mother and I looked at each other, stunned. This must have been the same young man who had been pulled off our excursion bus before leaving Romania only minutes after our luggage had been checked.

"I shudder to think what would have happened to us had they found our money in the camera spool, Mama."

"In His mercy, God saw fit to spare us that experience, honey. But my heart aches for this man and hundreds of others just like him all over the world who are persecuted under the mockery of so-called justice."

"Mama, can you imagine what a heart-wrenching feeling this must have been for him? If it was anything like what I experienced while waiting at the Turkish border when told we had to go back because we had no passports, it must have been dreadful. The question, though, which keeps ringing in my head over and over again is how come we made it and he didn't?"

"You may never have the answer to that question, Sperantza. Remember, we are finite human beings. What we see is only a glimpse in the grand scheme of life. There are many things in this life we do not understand. But, we must trust in the One who does—our Creator God, the Infinite One who 'never sleeps nor slumbers, who never leaves us, nor forsakes us.'

You and I are powerless to solve this young man's problem. But we know the One who can. Let's pray and ask God to help him. Not only him, but help all those hundreds and thousands around the globe who are persecuted tortured, lonely and hopeless.... He is the only One who can soothe their pain and give them hope."

Turning off the radio, we knelt beside the wooden chair, lifting our voice in prayer to our only source of strength, our Lord and Savior, Jesus Christ.

Suddenly, we heard a loud knock at the door.

"Hello Traian," said Mother opening it.

"Mrs. Totpal, we just returned from the Organization. They need you there as soon as possible—something about your Visa."

"You mean, today?"

"Yes, right away. They said it's urgent."

"Is there a problem," asked Mother?"

"They wouldn't say, Mrs. Totpal. All they told me is that they need you there immediately."

The trip to Rome that day felt like it took longer than ever before. I had butterflies in my stomach. I didn't know exactly how I felt, since both excitement and fear overwhelmed me. What would they say? What was the news? What if there were problems?

Then, I heard Mrs. Buonarroti tell Mother, "Mrs. Totpal, this morning we have received a telephone call from the American Embassy. Your entry Visa to the United States has been granted."

"What exactly does that mean?" asked Mother, her voice trembling.

"It means you will be able to leave for the United States as soon as we can make flight arrangements for you. I am calling Alitalia right now to see what availability they have. Once they give me a date, it's just a matter of them printing up the tickets delivering them to us, and you coming back to pick them up. Then, as they say, 'You'll be set to go.'" Mrs. Buonarroti must have seen the look of incredulity on Mother's face.

"Mrs. Totpal, it's true!" she said, smiling. "In just a few days, you will be heading to America."

THE ARRIVAL

Chapter 41

The morning of our departure had finally arrived. Entering the Leonardo Da Vinci Airport in Fiumicino was electrifying. The hustle and bustle of beeping horns, taxis, cars, and long accordion buses, as they made their way onto the large platforms to drop off and pick up passengers was a sight to behold as each drove with incredible precision within inches of each other.

As we entered the lobby, we passed a large group of people. Some spoke Russian, some Bulgarian, others Turkish, Polish... some Romanian. By the way they looked, I could tell they were just like us—immigrants in search of a better land.

Wrinkled babushkas, covered with colorful scarves, and trembling old men leaning on wooden canes were surrounded by worn, faded suitcases, tattered bags, and carton boxes tied with rope. Vibrant women and couples with children were there as well, awaiting with anticipation the moment when we would embark upon our journey to our new home—America— the country that has always stood as the symbol of freedom for all!

As my eyes scanned the scene, I knew my story, but couldn't help but wonder about theirs. What price had they paid? What sacrifice had they made to get to where they were this day? Who did they leave behind? And how long before they would see them again?

"Do you want to see our tickets?" Mother asked, interrupting my thoughts.

"Yes." I replied excitedly. "Do I have a window seat?"

"I can't tell yet, but we'll find out soon enough. They'll be letting us go to the gate in a few minutes since we're departing within an hour."

I couldn't wait to get on that plane. The excitement was mounting by the minute.

What would it feel like to travel across an ocean? What would it be like to see those hundred-story buildings, those famous skyscrapers I only read about? What about the people? What would it feel like to finally meet the American people?

"Your seats are 45 C and D," said the Alitalia flight attendant as we made our way into the massive airplane. It wasn't exactly by the window, but I was glad to be close enough to still see out. As Mother and I got situated, I kept watching the constant stream of people pouring in. From modern to dowdy, from confident to timid, the contrast between us immigrants and all the other travelers was clear.

It wasn't just the clothes that made the difference. Much more than that were the looks on their faces, which spoke a thousand words. The fear of the unknown, the pain, the suffering, the separation—those were the pictures reflected on those faces.

I wondered as I looked on, "What about me? What kind of story unfolds from my expression as people look at me? Will I ever fit in? Will I ever be an American?"

After the flight attendants checked our seatbelts and completed the required safety presentations, we were ready for take off. Even to this day, I stand amazed at how such a large steel bird filled with people and tons of luggage can fly through the air. But back then, having flown only once before, it was even more amazing. What made it more nerve-racking was knowing that we would be flying over water.

"Mama, I'm scared!" I finally uttered. "We'll be flying above the ocean. What if something happens? We would never see Daddy and Cornelia again."

"Darling, listen. Remember, God is with us! He's taken care of us so far. He won't leave us now. Just talk to Him, like you're talking to me."

Praying in my mind, I asked God to give me peace and take away my fears, then fell asleep.

I awoke to what I thought was the most delectable meal I had ever seen. "Oh, this looks delicious," I said, peeking through the wrapping. It looks like Osso Buco." I had been too nervous to eat anything that morning, but the aroma of the food emanating from the tray in front of me, not to mention the hunger pangs, enticed me to eat.

"I feel much better," I said to Mother. The flight has been really smooth, and we're almost half way, right?"

"Almost," said Mother, looking at her watch. "Do you see how God answered your prayer?"

But just as she finished those words, the captain came on announcing we were heading into a storm, and there would be strong turbulence.

"Keep your seatbelts on and remain seated," he said sternly.

The flight attendants rapidly took their seats. Within minutes, the plane began to shake from side to side. Then, it would dip into large air pockets, come up again, and then shake and dip down again and again as if it were a rag doll thrown upon the ocean waves.

My stomach was in knots. It felt like we were driving on huge boulders. The storm seemed to last for hours.

"Mama, I feel like throwing up," I finally said, turning towards her.

Her eyes were closed shut and her hands were tightly gripping the arm rests. I could tell she was praying.

"Mama, I'm scared," I said, shaking her, crying. The young woman seated beside us who, until then, had not uttered a single word, began to cry too.

"I'm scared, too!" she said looking to Mother as though she had the answer.

As Mother bit her upper lip and tried hard to hold back her tears, she replied, "Pray, let's pray."

Right then and there, Mother began praying, pleading with God to calm our souls and stop the storm. There was no time to think about whether or not what she was about to do was appropriate or even acceptable. Mother did what she knew she could do! What she always did—turn to her only source of strength—her God, her Anchor and her Rock.

Although the storm continued for a while, the terror and fear that had gripped us to that point was squelched. Sweet peace came in its place.

"Th... Thank you ma'am," whispered the young girl to Mother, wiping off her tears. "I can't say I believe in God, but I can see you do. No doubt He heard your prayer."

"Where are you from?" asked Mother, able to finally breathe a sigh of relief as the storm quieted down.

"From Brașov."

"So are we!" And thus ensued a conversation that continued for a couple more hours, until we saw... her. It was the captain who pointed her out.

There she stood!

Tall and beautiful, looking larger than life, arm lifted up, holding its ever lasting flame, welcoming into her harbor the pilgrims of the world. Although the years had aged her, the tempests raged about her, and elements had worn her, she still remains faithful at her post. Dignified, unshaken, and unmoved even by the evil of this world, she stands alone as the symbol of liberty for an entire world to see!

The Lady—Lady Liberty!

As she came into full view, it seemed as though the entire plane burst into applause. There must have been lots and lots of us, immigrants there, because the sound of our hands clapping made it feel as if the whole plane was shaking with excitement. And then, as though in perfect unison, we all exclaimed, "America! America! America!"

Chapter 42

What a journey this had been, from the country I once knew to the one I could only imagine... America! From my birthplace to my new-found heart place!

Eight long, difficult months had passed since Mother and I had set foot on American soil. Appeal after appeal and memorandum after memorandum, begging and pleading for the reunification of our family left both, Mama and I exhausted, but not hopeless. We knew, without a doubt, that the God of Heaven and Earth would somehow make a way for our family to be together again one day.

On August 13, 1980, more than one year after we had been separated from our loved ones, Mama and I, together with Auntie Lia and Uncle Nicu and friends, were heading to the LAX Airport in Los Angeles, California. I remember that evening, as if it were yesterday.

Even though the drive from Loma Linda to Los Angeles had been long, I was beaming. Walking up to the gate, I made my way close to the window. I pressed my nose against it as my eyes searched the night sky for the arrival of the airplane that carried our precious cargo. I saw lights slowly approaching.

"That's them! That's them! They're here! They're here!" I shouted. Turning around, I saw my aunt holding my mother tightly.

"Don't cry, Mama. Don't cry! They're here!" I said, thinking I could keep it together.

As the airplane came to a full stop and people began getting off, our eyes were fixed upon that door. I felt like my heart would pop out of my chest because it was beating so fast. Person after person got off, but not Daddy! "I know they're here, but why aren't they coming out?" I thought. "What's taking them so long?"

After the last person got off the airplane, in between the flight attendants and airplane personnel who were walking out, we saw him. His arms were tightly wrapped around a sleepy little girl, carrying her ever-so-tenderly as he slowly made his way out.

"Daddy! Daddy! Daddy!" I screamed, running towards him. With my eyes blinded by my tears, I almost made him stumble.

He didn't speak. He couldn't. He just sobbed uncontrollably. Held tightly in his arms, we all stood there for I-don't-even-know-how-long. Wrapped in the warmth of his embrace, our emotions and our tears, which had been bottled up for oh, so long, finally gave way, washing over us until we had no more.

And then, as if watching a scene play in slow motion, I saw Mama extend her arms toward her little girl who, until that moment, had been firmly glued around her Daddy's neck. She didn't move. She just looked, and looked at Mother for a while, her chocolate, marble eyes searching her face intently, as if to say: "I think I know you, but it has been so long.... Why did you leave me? Why?"

Being separated from my family for thirteen months felt like forever, even for me, but, for a four-year-old, it must have felt like an eternity.

"It's Mommy, darling. It's Mommy," Mother said, trying to reassure her, reaching for her once again. But her request was met with the same expression as before. "Do I know you? Why did you leave me? Why?" Mother began to weep as she continued calling her little girl.

"Sweetheart, it's Mommy! It's Mommy! Please let me touch you! Let me hold you, please. Mommy will never leave you again..."

Standing there, watching the scene unfold before my very eyes, my heart just ached, remembering the pain I saw on Mother's face as she kissed her little girl goodbye the morning we had left Romania. For more than a year, Mother had cried, prayed, and hoped for this moment to arrive. Now, it had come, but oh, at what a price...

Chapter 43

I don't remember sleeping that night when we got home. As we sat around the table, we all waited anxiously to finally hear the truth about what really happened to Daddy after we escaped.

"The day the two of you were to return," said Father, "I went and waited anxiously for the bus. I didn't know if you had made it, but I had told myself I would be calm, no matter what. But when the motor coach pulled in and everybody got off but you, I felt a sense of desperation come over me like never before. As reality hit, I feared I was going to loose my mind. I couldn't think. I couldn't speak. I just stood there, shocked, until the tour guide approached me.

'Mr. Totpal, I am so sorry,' she said, 'but we don't know what happened with your wife and daughter. We were together until the last day of our trip when we separated for the Bazaar. We instructed everybody to meet us back at the hotel at 1:00 PM and told them we would wait another 30 minutes for late-comers. Your wife and daughter never returned. We waited four more hours and called several major hospitals in the area thinking they might have gotten into an accident. We don't know what has happened to them.'

Hearing that, made me feel even more desperate. 'What if you had been in an accident? What if you didn't make it? What if something horrible had happened to you?'

Feeling utterly helpless, I said, 'Mrs. Ionescu, you don't understand. I have a four-year-old I must take care of. I need my wife. I need my child. Please, let me speak to the Securitate agent who traveled on this trip.'

'There were no Securitate agents on this trip, Mr. Totpal,' she responded, sternly. 'There never are!'

'Are you telling me that you would allow a group of tourists to enter a democratic country without a Securitate agent to assure their return? I must speak with them at once.'"

"Were you not afraid to speak to them like that?" asked Mother.

"I don't know what came over me. But I was not scared of them anymore. 'I must speak to someone now,' I told her. 'I need my wife. I can't live without her. I'll go to Turkey. I'll go wherever she is, but I can't live without her.'

I felt like I was loosing my mind. As hard as it had been living under the Communist regime, we at least had each other. We were together. Nothing could have prepared me for that day—nothing!

The anguish of not knowing whether you were dead or alive, not knowing if or when I would ever see you again, made me act like a mad man. Those people must have thought I was a lunatic. If it hadn't been for God and your parents, who helped me cope through this ordeal, I would have never made it.

When I finally heard from you several days later and knew you were alive, it was as if a huge boulder had been lifted off my chest. But the shock impacted me so deeply, that it left me hospitalized for weeks. The hardest thing for me was to tell our little girl that you weren't coming back."

"How did you possibly do that?" asked Mother, with tears in her eyes.

"I reminded her again and again about how much you loved her. I told her that you went to find a better place for us to live. And then I kept assuring her that Jesus would help us to be together again.

What I never expected, from our four-year-old was her reply:

'If Mommy loves me, Daddy, why did she only take Sperantza? Why did she leave me?'

How could I possibly answer that? The only thing I could do was pray and ask God to give me the strength I needed to face another day.

As I began the process of reunification, I went to those offices every single week, sometimes two or three times a week, begging, pleading, asking them to allow me to leave. I did all that while still trying to make a living, taking care of the house, the business, and myself.

In the beginning, the Communists told me to divorce you. 'Marry someone else,' they said. When they realized I wasn't going to give up and got bombarded by your appeals and memorandums, they finally relented. But not without a price..."

"Our house?" asked Mother.

"It's gone."

"And the business?" she continued.

"That too. The car, the cameras, the house, the studio, it's all gone," Father said.

"So, we have nothing left?" I found myself asking aloud.

"No, honey," Daddy responded. "But what we do have now is far more precious than what we've ever had—because we have each other and we have freedom.

Four years old, with my mother.

Relaxing with Tata and Buni on the verandah.

Posing for a picture with Mother and Buni.

Taking my baby sister, Cornelia
for a stroll in her new carriage.

Celebrating my sister's first birthday
three years before our escape.

Glimpses of Brașov, Romania...

...the city we lived in.

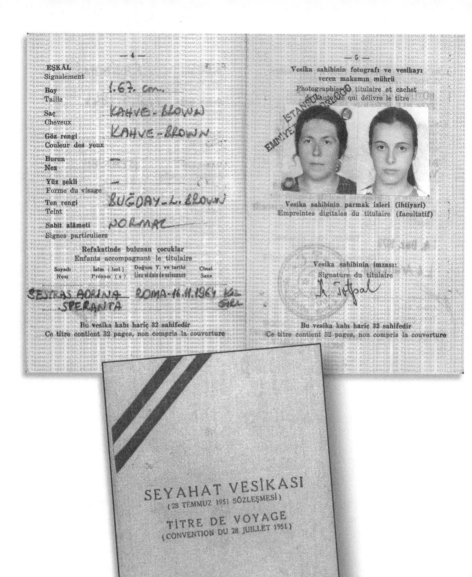

Our travel document from Istanbul, Turkey.

Arriving in the United States
and reunited with my aunt and uncle.

My parents
Michaela and Corneliu Totpal, 2010

With my sister, Cornelia, 2010

20 YEARS LATER

Chapter 44

N oel, I have an emergency! The satellite dish for *Hope 2000* is stuck in Miami. I need you to hand deliver it to Romania," I overheard Ralph Ringer tell my boss.

"What? Romania? Ralph, I don't need to go to Romania, but Adriana does. Adriana!"

Hearing my middle name being called, I jumped to my feet and dashed into my director's office.

"Yes, Noel."

"Ralph, tell Adriana what's going on, please."

Evangelism Coordinator for Florida Conference of Seventh-day Adventists, Ralph was one of the kindest, Christ-like pastors I had ever worked with in my life. But that day, there was much urgency in his voice when he said, "Adriana, we have a problem! Seven hundred pounds worth of satellite equipment for the *Hope 2000* series is stuck in Miami. We can't send it via cargo. It won't make it on time. We need someone to accompany it to Romania for the evangelistic series that is about to begin. Are you willing to help?"

"When would I need to leave?"

"I'm not sure yet. Pastor Brad Thorp from ACN (Adventist Communication Network) will call me back in a few minutes to give me more details. He called from Romania asking me to help, but I just got back from India. I can't go. That's why I asked Noel, but he suggested you."

This felt surreal. Just earlier that morning, while getting dressed, I had whispered a prayer, "Lord, I know this is impossible, but if it were possible, I'd love to go to Romania! I want to personally invite my family to hear Your message of love for them. Maybe this time, they'll come."

Throughout the years I had worked with Pastor Noel Shanko, I had shared the burden I carried in my heart for my extended family who lived so far away, to one day come to know Jesus. As Ministerial Secretary for the Florida Conference, he and I spoke often of the mysterious ways God uses to reach those we cannot.

It was clear that day, that Pastor Shanko had never forgotten. Waking up from my reverie, I responded, "I'll call my husband."

"Ronnie, listen, there is an emergency situation, and I may need to travel to Romania for *Hope 2000*—something about the satellite dish. The details are sketchy right now, but would you be opposed to me going?"

"When would that be?" came the answer.

"Maybe in two or three days."

"Honey, if they need your help, how can I say no? You must go wherever God calls!"

"Thank you, Ronnie! I'll keep you posted as soon as I know more."

No sooner had I hung up the phone, I heard my name being called again.

"Adriana, quick, in my office. It's Brad Thorp," said Ralph. I dashed in and picked up the receiver.

"This is Adriana!"

"Adriana, Pastor Thorp here, calling from Romania. I understand you're willing to help us."

"Yes, Pastor, when would I need to leave?"

"Today. You must catch the four o'clock plane for Frankfurt, leaving from Miami."

"But it's already noon, and I'm still in Orlando."

"I know," Pastor Thorp responded. "I asked Ralph to find a flight for you to Miami as soon as possible. That's the only way you can make it since driving would not get you there on time. Listen, do you understand the magnitude of what we are asking you to do?"

"Yes, sir, I believe I do."

"Very well, then, I will contact the cargo agent in Miami and ask him to wait for you at the Lufthansa desk. He will assist you with the equipment. It's big—700 hundred pounds worth of big!

"I've made a tentative reservation for you for the four o'clock flight from Miami to Bucharest. I will call back to confirm it. Please write down this record identification number and present it to the Lufthansa desk when you get there. They will locate you in the computer and print out the ticket for you.

Oh, Adriana, one more thing. Every time you change planes, you must be sure the equipment travels with you and is not left behind. You must not leave without it! You will also need enough cash on hand for any surcharges, not to mention the taxes when you get to Bucharest. The equipment is worth nearly 100,000 dollars."

I felt my head was spinning. "Sir," I finally said, "I need you to pray for me."

"Adriana, we will begin praying immediately and will not stop until we see you here safe and sound with the equipment. Be assured of that. May God be with you!"

As I hung up the phone and stepped out of Ralph's office, I saw him motion to me as he hung up the phone at my desk. I felt like we were playing musical chairs.

"Adriana, you must catch the two o'clock flight to Miami to make the four o'clock to Frankfurt. Here's your reservation," he said, handing me a piece of paper.

"While you were on the phone, I got approval from our president for your travel overseas. I'm getting a check cut as we speak. I'll be running to the bank to cash it. I will then meet you at your home. In case I miss you, I'll catch you at the airport. You need this money. Hurry! It's already 12:30."

"I need to call Ronnie," I heard myself say out loud. "He thinks I'm leaving in several days!"

I called my husband and blurted, "Ronnie, honey, I can't explain. I need you to go home and pack for me. I'm leaving in an hour."

"What? What happened?"

"Please, I can't explain. Just go. Pack me a couple of suits and some shoes. Don't forget my passport. See you at home."

The trip home that normally took 15 minutes, I made in seven! When I arrived, my husband had already begun the process and was literally dumping the contents of entire drawers into my luggage. He looked as frazzled as I felt.

"I'll explain what happened on our way to the airport," I reassured him. "What about my passport, do you have it?"

"Yes, on the table."

"We've got to go. If not, I'll miss this plane. It's more than 45 minutes to the airport and it's almost one o'clock. Oh, the money! Pastor Ralph's not here and I need the cash."

"Can't you pay with a credit card?"

"No, not in Romania, not with those airport agents."

I placed my passport in my purse, I opened the door and nearly stumbled over Pastor Ralph.

"You're here! Thank God!"

"I was just about to ring the doorbell when you opened." He handed me the money and added, "I hope this will be enough. Please be careful! Adriana, I know what we've asked you to do is not easy. But remember, this is God's mission. His meetings! His satellite! He will be with you every step of the way. We will be praying for you."

We stood next to our car with the motor running, anxious to leave, but paused a few more minutes to pray and ask God's blessing and protection. Just when we were about to pull away, Pastor Ralph motioned us to stop.

"Now what?" I thought.

"It must be important Sperantza, otherwise he wouldn't stop us when he knows we're running against time."

"But, we've got to go," I said exasperated.

"I know. Be patient, Sperantza."

"It's past 1:00 o'clock."

Waiting for him to finish his cell phone conversation, made seconds feel like hours.

"That was Brad Thorp," Pastor Ralph said. Thank God he caught us. The identity record number he gave you for the Lufthansa flight was incorrect. Without it, they would have had no way of finding you in the computer in Miami. This is the one you need," he said, handing me a piece of paper with the number written on it. As I grabbed it, I breathed a sigh of relief. "Thank you, Pastor." And with that, we sped off.

We arrived at the Orlando Airport ten minutes before boarding. If it hadn't been for my husband carrying my bag and running to the gate, I doubt I would have made it. This was two years before the 9/11 tragedy, and we could still enjoy the liberties that we no longer have.

I approached the desk nearly out of breath. "May I have an attendant assist me when I land in Miami? I asked. "My connecting flight to Frankfurt is with Lufthansa. I need help with several pieces of cargo that I must locate before departure."

"Sure, no problem. I'll put in the request for you," the young lady answered.

"When you get to Miami, there will be a Delta agent who will accompany you to the Lufthansa desk and assist you with your luggage."

"Thanks. What's the scheduled arrival time, please?

"2:50 p.m."

"Hopefully that gives me enough time..." I thought.

I chose the aisle seat on the right, near the front as I boarded the small prop plane. "I'll be the first one to get out," I reasoned. "That way, no one can hold me back."

Although quite heavy and voluminous, I literally dragged my garment bag with no wheels on to the plane with me, just so I could avoid any delays. My mind felt like it was going a million miles a minute.

I finally closed my eyes and breathed a short prayer. "Lord, please help me. Help me find that equipment. Help me catch the plane. Help me get there on time."

The more I prayed, the longer the trip seemed to take.

"Are we circling the airport," I finally asked?

"Yes, we have no clearance for landing yet," the flight attendant answered.

Desperate to know the time, I was getting ready to pull up my sleeve and look at my watch.

"Don't look at your watch!"

"What?" I thought.

"Don't look at your watch!"

What I heard was not an audible voice, by any means, but it was such a strong impression, that I decided to obey.

After the fourth time circling the airport, the plane finally landed. I bolted out of there as fast as I could, my eyes desperately seeking the promised Delta agent, who was nowhere to be found. There was no agent waiting for me at the gate. No assistant, no one to help. I picked up my heavy garment bag and began running toward the main terminal. I had no clue where I was going. No clue where the Lufthansa desk was. After a few minutes, I passed a digital clock that read 3:27 PM. My flight to Frankfurt was scheduled to leave in exactly 33 minutes.

Suddenly, I felt all my strength leave me. I stopped. Having no more power to carry my bag, I stood there as though paralyzed. A few steps away I saw an empty cart. I threw my garment bag on it and continued running. "Where is Lufthansa? Where is Lufthansa, please?" I kept asking out loud.

"To the right, underneath the stairways," someone finally answered.

Exhausted, I arrived at the Lufthansa Desk. It was 3:45 PM.

Chapter 45

I'm here to pick up 700 pounds of equipment for the four o'clock Frankfurt flight," I blurted out, barely breathing.

"Excuse me?" came the response.

"Just a moment," I said, catching my breath. "I'm here to pick up some cargo equipment I am to accompany on the four o'clock Frankfurt flight and then on to Romania."

"Your name, please."

"Sperantza Adriana Pasos."

"While I locate this cargo, the counter agent will further assist you," he said, pointing to the nearby stern-looking woman.

"Your passport and I.D. locator number."

As she looked them over, she said matter-of-factly: "Your name on your passport does not match your reservation name. I need a correct I.D." My heart sank. I remembered I had never changed my passport from my maiden name to my married name.

"Madam, you can see this is me. Look, here are my ministerial credentials. They have my married name on them. And this is my driver's license. It does, too.

"Sorry. That's not enough. I need a copy of your marriage certificate, otherwise you won't be able to get on this flight. That's the policy."

"I need to get on this flight," I replied. "I must get on this flight. I'm telling you this is me. You can see this is me."

"I'm sorry!" she responded coldly.

Determined not to take no for an answer, I asked to speak to a manager.

"There," she motioned, right back to the gentleman who had first helped me.

Having apparently overheard our conversation, he said, "Add her maiden name to the ticket, please."

"Thank you sir," I muttered.

"I finally located the equipment for you," he said. They're bringing it up the elevator momentarily."

When I turned around, I saw several enormous boxes placed on two huge cargo carts pushed by four men.

"Are you Adriana Pasos?"

"Yes sir, I am."

"Please sign here," he said. "Enclosed is all the paperwork for the satellite dish. Ten boxes in all."

"$100,000.00 worth of equipment," I thought. "This is insane. How will I ever get this through the Romanian customs? Not to mention the taxes they'll charge me for this. They will be on to me like wolves on a fresh trail of blood."

"You won't make that flight," the stern woman behind the counter said, interrupting my thoughts. "You still have to go through customs."

"Sir," I said, addressing myself directly to the manager, ignoring her completely, "I must make this flight. This equipment must get to Romania. I don't even need to go, but the equipment must. It's crucial. It's for an evangelistic campaign and it must get there. Please help me!"

"Madam, will you have any problems in Romania with all this satellite equipment?"

"No sir. I'll have no problems in Romania. Just please get me to that plane."

Looking at the men who stood next to the cargo carts, the manager said, "Gentlemen, since these boxes are sealed, bypass customs and take this equipment directly to the plane."

"Did I hear him right?" I thought. "Did he just say what I thought he said?"

"Madam, here's your boarding pass to Frankfurt and on to Romania."

"Thank you, sir, thank you," I said nervously.

"Sir, the gate? Where's the gate? Will I still make it? Do they know I'm coming?"

"Madam, you must hurry, but you must not panic!"

"Panic," I thought. "If you only knew that I've been panicked for several hours now."

"Underneath the staircase, past the escalator to the right, Gate number 7, I heard him say."

"Thank you, sir," I said, running as fast as I could towards the gate.

I saw the gateway door was still open. I flashed the ticket to the assistant and ran down the gangway into the plane, nearly colliding into the flight attendant who was waiting to close the door. As I entered the Airbus, I found my seat near the center aisle and sank down into it, completely exhausted.

Chapter 46

Although my body had no strength, my mind still raced. I captured the events of that day into the notebook I had pulled out. My thoughts flowed on to the paper as vertiginously as an avalanche detaching from a mountaintop. When I finally put down my pen, I sensed my shoulders relax a bit and slowly drifted into sleep.

It was early, the following morning that I arrived in Germany. My flight to Bucharest was not for another five hours. As I walked the long, wide corridors, I found my way to the gate and spotted an agent.

"Excuse me please, can you tell me what time the desk will open for the departing flight to Bucharest, Romania?"

"Can't you see I'm trying to work?" came the response. "It's because of people like you who constantly interrupt me that I can't do my job."

"Forgive me," I said, walking away. "Oh, Lord," I thought, "please don't let this be the person who's going to work the Bucharest flight."

One hour before my flight was to depart, the desk personnel changed. "Thank you God," I whispered.

Handing my ticket and passport to the new agent, I greeted her cheerfully in English, "Good morning."

"Good morning," came the reply, accompanied by the most beautiful smile.

Encouraged by her pleasant demeanor, I said, "Madam, I really need your help. I am accompanying several large pieces of equipment to Romania, and I need to make sure they are on the plane with me. How can I know they will be transferred from my connecting flight?"

"Our system is 99 percent accurate. If there is a problem it should pop up on my screen," she said, pointing to her computer.

"But there is still a one percent chance that it won't make it, right?"

"Yes, there is. I'll tell you what," she continued. "You wait here until everybody boards. If something comes up, I can tell you."

I stepped aside and waited patiently, praying silently until the last passenger boarded.

"Nothing yet," she said, smiling, "but you will need to board now. Best of luck to you."

I left the gate area and made my way to my seat, waiting for the plane to take off, right on time. This was Germany, after all. But, to my surprise, it didn't. Within minutes, the captain made the following announcement in German, Spanish, and English, "Ladies and gentlemen, we apologize for the delay but we've had some unexpected large pieces of cargo that are being loaded unto the plane right now. As soon as that is completed, we will be taking off. We apologize for the inconvenience."

I felt like standing up and shouting from the top of my lungs, "That's my equipment! That's my equipment! God, You are so awesome!" Since I sensed however, that not everyone would have appreciated my enthusiasm, I chose to silently say: "Thank You God! Not only are You taking care of this for me, but You are making sure I know You're doing it."

Chapter 47

Since I had experienced all of those miracles along the way, I thought, "Surely, I have nothing to be concerned about in Romania." But, as the plane was nearing its final approach, I felt fear's ugly claws tightening like a vice around my heart.

"Lord, what now? How in the world will I pass through customs? I only have $2,000 in cash, and that's not nearly enough to cover the taxes they'll want to charge me. Not if I give them the paper declaring the value as $100,000." Even though returning as an American citizen, scary memories of my distant past came flooding back. "What if they stop me? What do I say? What do I do?"

Approaching the window that read Visas, I handed my passport to the agent. He stamped it, and I proceeded to the baggage claim, waiting for the carousel to begin unloading.

I glanced toward the exit and saw a sign above one door that read: *Nothing to Declare*. "That's it." I thought. "I'm going through the *Nothing to Declare* gate! "I'm going to pull that cargo right behind me," I decided. "And

God, You're going to have to blind them, because I'm not stopping until I get this equipment out of here and to its final destination."

Just as those thoughts crossed through my mind, I noticed several men pull the equipment off the carousel and load it onto large carts. I looked to verify the number of each package when I saw another hand near mine doing the same.

"Are you from the Media Center?" the voice with a heavy accent asked.

"Yes, I am," I replied.

"Wait here. Do not show paper, please. I be back in a moment," he said in broken English.

Five minutes later, this chubby, medium-height man, came back.

"Let's go," he said.

I followed him. Here I was, walking out of the Baneasa International Airport, bypassing all military personnel, police, and customs with several men behind me pulling and pushing nearly 1,000 pounds of satellite equipment through the *Nothing to Declare* gate and no one stopped me. No one questioned me. No one asked me for money. This was a miracle! How great of a miracle it was, I would learn in detail, only the following day.

"My name is Daniel, and I am a seminary student," he finally said in Romanian, relieved to know I spoke the language. "Please wait here. There is a van that will be transporting the equipment to the Congress Hall. You'll be coming with me in another car."

"I'm not leaving this equipment out of my sight," I said. "Wherever it goes, I go."

"No, no, you do not understand. We will go together. But the equipment cannot fit in my car. Look at the size of it," he said pointing to his tiny Renault.

I kept my eye on that van all the way to the Congress Hall. As we parked and I got out, I breathed a sigh of relief, knowing we had arrived and my mission was almost complete.

"Adriana, thank God you're here!"

"Pastor Finley! Teenie! It's so nice to see you, both!"

"Call Pastor Thorp" said Teenie. "Let's tell him you're here. He's been leading a prayer chain and promised he wouldn't stop until he saw you come through those doors."

"You've made it. Praise God! And through the *Nothing to Declare* gate I hear. This is a miracle. Especially, since for the past two weeks we have been struggling with the Romanian Customs to release 12 English Bibles we have sent for our translators and have not yet succeeded.

"Pastor Thorp, it is so nice to meet you," I responded.

Looking at his watch, he asked: "What time is it? Mine is still on Eastern time.

"Six o'clock" came the response.

"You know what's even more amazing?" he continued, "We needed 24 hours to install the satellite dish and get it ready for tomorrow night at 7:00. God gave us an extra hour to spare."

Chapter 48

Exhausted, I had planned to crash in my hotel room till the following morning. I had been up for the past 36 hours, and the emotional impact of the trip had worn me out.

But Daniel, the Theology student who had picked me up from the airport, was so excited to introduce me to his wife that I couldn't refuse.

"You must attend the VIP meeting tonight," he said.

"I wasn't planning on it," I responded. "I am so tired."

"You cannot miss it. Some great dignitaries will be there tonight," he urged. "Please go rest for an hour and then my wife and I will come to pick you up."

I was almost dizzy from exhaustion as I made my way to the hotel room. I knew if I were to lay down, I would have difficulty waking up. Instead, I chose to take an invigorating shower, which rejuvenated me for the rest of the evening. Then I joined Daniel and Laura for the VIP meeting and an experience I would never forget.

"That is Father Mihail from the Orthodox Metropoly," he said discreetly. "The gentleman on the right is the first Romanian cosmonaut who flew into space. The assistant to the president is here tonight as well."

"As in, Romanian President?" I asked incredulously.

"Yes, His Excellency could not make it due to a previous commitment, so he sent his assistant instead. Men of great accomplishment, poets, authors, and well-known lecturers and orators have been invited here tonight. They have been intrigued by the Health Symposium held for the past several weeks and want to hear more."

"So, the Health Symposium must have been the kickoff for the upcoming evangelistic campaign," I thought, as I followed Daniel and his wife up the immense marble stairs.

Entering into a large room covered with immense Persian rugs and upholstered armchairs of plush burgundy velour, I was lead to a seat towards the front. After the necessary formalities and introductions, Pastor Mark Finley, speaker for the *It Is Written*, International Television Program, took the platform.

"Illustrious dignitaries, most honorable guests, ladies and gentlemen, good evening! For the past several days, you have enjoyed our Health Symposium which tackled some of the challenges you face as a nation and vital issues that impact your health and your lives. It is about one of those issues that I would like to speak to you tonight—the element of stress.

"As men and women in such positions of leadership, importance and great responsibility, you can, no doubt, relate. You carry the weight of an entire country on your shoulders, and the decisions you must make are often difficult ones. Stress is an intricate part of your lives, but I want to tell you, that is good news! I say that because it means you are alive. Only dead people have no stress.

Tonight, however, I want to share with you the only key that will help you relieve it, so that stress doesn't harm you, but empower you, instead.

An experiment was done by scientists some time ago to measure how animals coped with stress. They took a baby lamb and placed it alone in a pen. At the opposite end, they placed a bowl of food.

When the baby lamb, who had been previously wired for the experiment became hungry and approached the bowl of food, the experts sent electrical impulses to his body. They then measured his stress level. Shocked and scared, the lamb retreated rapidly into a corner, remaining there until he was hungry again.

When he approached the bowl of food, he once again received the electrical shocks. And once more, he retreated back into a corner. The experts continued the process and monitored his increasing stress level, until the baby lamb became so overwhelmed his heart gave out.

The experts then, took another baby lamb and placed it in the same pen with the same bowl of food, but this time along with his mother. They wired him just as they did the previous one, and when the lamb went to eat, he was shocked just as the other one had been. Scared, the baby lamb retreated to his mother. There was a dialogue between the two of them, but then the baby lamb went back to eat. Shocked by the electrical impulses, he once again ran to his mother.

Again, there was a dialogue, and again the baby lamb went back to eat. What the experts finally concluded was that even though they continued shocking him, the baby lamb was able to cope with his stress.

I ask you tonight, what made the difference? The difference, ladies and gentlemen, was his mother. That baby lamb had someone who loved him, someone he could run to, someone to comfort him, someone to encourage him and tell him to go on.

And you know what? In the Good Book, it says that you and I also have Someone we can run to. His name is Jesus Christ! When we are stressed, when our lives seem to make no sense, when the world seems to crumble under our very feet, He is there. When our children are sick, our finances are in a mess, when a loved one dies, or someone we love abandons us, He is still there. He promises to never leave you, nor forsake you!

Tonight, He stands with opened arms, inviting you to come. He is the true and only answer to your stress! 'Come to me,' He says, 'all of you who are heavy laden and heavy burdened and I will give you rest.' "

Suddenly, sitting there, listening to Pastor Mark Finley speak, a feeling of such overwhelming gratitude came over me that I began to cry. It had been twenty years ago that Mother and I had escaped this place so we could freely worship God.

And now, in the very hallways where, years before, Dictator Nicolae Ceauşescu had shouted and imposed his Marxist ideology, claiming that God did not exist, now stood a man who preached the Gospel of Freedom! The very place where orders had been given to persecute and kill believers had now become the platform where Jesus Christ was lifted up. It was an unbelievable moment—one I will cherish for the rest of my life.

That night, seated amidst the dignitaries of an entire country, I felt that history had come full circle, and I was privileged enough to experience it.

About The Author

Speerantza Adriana Pasos is an inspirational writer and speaker. Her greatest passion is to share hope with those she encounters and the reassurance that we have been created for a purpose much greater than any one of us can imagine.

She currently works for Florida Hospital, a faith-based organization ranked one of America's Best and largest admitting hospitals, where she serves the ministry of Spiritual Ambassadors within Mission Development.

Traveling, foreign languages, gourmet cooking and spending time with her precious family are some of the things she enjoys most.

She lives in Orlando, Florida with her husband, Ronald, an architect, and beautiful daughters, Gabriella and Evangelina.

For more information please visit www.hopeinpresentdanger.com.

To plan a speaking engagement, connect with the author
or obtain copies of this book visit
www.hopeinpresentdanger.com
or write
Always Hope
P.O. Box 162303
Altamonte Springs, FL 32716-2303